ASIA360

ASIA³⁶⁰

The culture of building businesses in Asia

Phil Kelly

Writers Club Press

San Jose New York Lincoln Shanghai

Asia^{360}
The culture of building businesses in Asia

Writers Club Press
an imprint of iUniverse.com, Inc.

For information address:
iUniverse.com, Inc.
5220 S 16th, Ste. 200
Lincoln, NE 68512
www.iuniverse.com

ISBN: 0-595-17447-7

Printed in the United States of America

Dedicated to…

Ashley
Jake and
Nicholas Kelly
who fill my life
with love and laughter,
pride and motivation…

Contents

Acknowledgments

As I write this, I am once again standing at the door of a new adventure. Just after beginning this book I left Dell to go out on my own into yet another start-up, still in Asia, but this time with my own business in the exciting new frontier of the Internet. The most recent change and challenge, like the book, wouldn't be possible without the support, encouragement, guidance and friendship I've experienced on every step of the journey, from the moment I first set foot on Asian soil and continuing to this day.

My gratitude is extended to many people who have affected, shared and influenced my life. Originally I had written a much longer acknowledgement, with specific comments and thanks...however as I read it many times over, it just did not seem complete or adequate enough, as all were/are very important for different reasons at different stages of my life. So I have chosen to mention many, and will extend my gratitude to each personally. Thank you:

...Phil and Barbara Kelly; Pat and Seana Kelly and all of my family members; Samantha and A.J.; Monica Lau and Charles; Dennis and Sheila Smith; Mark Stevens; James Root; Ranjan Marwah; Chip Longley; Jean Salata; Stephen Stonefield; Moses Tsang; Stewart Homler; Jack Poon; Alex Arena; Norman Yuen; President Fidel Ramos; Chief Minister Koh; Ron Greenwell; Terry Jaron; Stan DeCosmo; Gay Hendricks; Laura Joyce; Michael Dell; Mort Topfer; David Bernstein; Gary Elliott; Keith and Kathy Goodenough; Buddy and Maureen Griffin; Jim and Shelley Hulihan; John Legere; Kate Ludeman; Tom Meredith; Tom Green; Martyn Ratcliffe; Kevin Rollins; Larry Sloven;

Braden Waverley; Jerry and Connie Thompkins; Ooi-Wong Wai-kin; Paula Athye; Michael Bearer; Jack Cantillon; Diane Chan; Alex Chu; Andie Chan; Byron Chan; David Chan; Peter Chan; Aun Gim Tan; Theresa Goh; Bob Greenberg; Eric Harslem; Steve Haslett; Ed Ho; Marty and Kirsten Jacobvitz; Dawn Kleinman; Deborah Li; Gershon Norwitz; Curtis Olson; Charlie Parker; Dick Rigsby; Siva Parkash Shanmugan; Jo Lynn Smith; S.P. Tan; C.S. Tang; Poh Lin Teoh; Lee Choo Tiat; Neile Wolfe; Simon Wong; C.S. Yue; Ernie Tate; Dan Russell; Jim King; Peter Sykes; Harry Cousens; Darryl Lim; Dick Lee; Chip Saunders; Jerry Gregoire; Angelina Foo; Jingle Panigbatan; Gerrit Heyns; Rebecca Sui; Rosaline Chow Koo; Peter Steel; Bill DeKruif; Pedro Ng; Jay Davis; Eva Chen; Jennifer Yuen; Prithvi Shergill; Russ Passarella; Chi Luu; Ron Ramos; Fook Keong Ching; Timothy Hui; TK Chiang; James Harris; Andrew Chua; Jim Hildebrandt; John Gilette; Karen Pump; Mark Blacker; Matt Burledge; Frank Au; Rich Chappelear; Steve Turkowiak; Susan Crast; Rob Nelson; Sam Hildebrant; Susan Burton; Tommy Lam; Peter Mills; Steve Foland; Ken Chow; Joe Tucci;

While the list of those who deserve thanks for their generosity is infinite, my memory is not. If I have overlooked anyone, it is with apologies and then hope that my gratitude is known, nonetheless, to all of my many colleagues, friends and acquaintances, mentioned and not, from the past and present—and still ahead on the road. My appreciation is profound.

Lastly, a special thank you to Laura Joyce, Mylinh Lee, Jennifer Yuen and Jack Poon for their assistance with this book.

Introduction

Eight years ago, I set off on an adventure into a new frontier. That may strike you as overly dramatic, or maybe you don't think the words *business* and *adventure* could ever have much to do with each other. After all, business is work, and adventure is something you do when the work is all done. Adventure (but never business!) is play: exciting, challenging, ever-shifting, never dull. Right?

Wrong.

See business as an adventure—particularly when it involves starting up a new enterprise in a foreign culture—which is why I've written this book. You can find books about adapting to foreign cultures, and you can find books about adapting your product to fit into a foreign market. There's a business start-up book for every letter of the alphabet and then some, and they all have something in common: They're business books—unmistakably, no-question-about-it, forget-casual-Fridays business books. There's nothing wrong with that, of course. This is a business book, too. But it's also something more. This is a business-as-adventure book, a book laying out not only the how-tos of Asia-Pacific start-up, but also the why-nots. Why not adapt to your host culture rather than expect it to adapt to you? Why not go into the start-up with the mind-set of a pioneer, an adventurer, a risk-taker exploring the last frontier? And here's the kicker, the "why-not" that sets this book apart from the rest: Why not have *fun* starting up your business in the Asia-Pacific?

Imagine yourself as a foot soldier cutting through the heavy underbrush in an uninhabited land, creating something new, with easier access for those who come along behind you. Imagine yourself as a person of uncommon courage going into undiscovered territory—the first, the one willing to take the risk—trying to build a base from which you will live your adventure, and from which others will learn. Imagine yourself as Neil Armstrong, one foot on the step of *Apollo 11* and the other connecting with the dusty surface of the moon for the first time; Magellan exploring the Philippines; Lewis and Clark cutting a swath through the west; or an immigrant arriving at Ellis Island with nothing but guts and an unwavering desire to make something better of himself and his new home.

Now imagine this: Your job description may have you heading up the new Asian division of the most successful widgetmaker in the United States, but you're not just one of the suits at corporate. What you really are is a pioneer, and you're about to enter the final frontier.

In 1994, in my second year as Vice-President and General Manager for Motorola in North Asia, I was recruited to join Dell Computer Corporation. I soon received my marching orders from the higher-ups at Dell: Start a division of Dell in the Asia-Pacific. Like we all do when we get new projects, I read between the lines, and the message was clear: Build it and make it work!

We weren't going into the Asia-Pacific to conduct a social experiment to see how well Dell got along in another culture, and we weren't expanding just to list another field office on our letterhead. We were going into the region because someone at Dell—a lot of someones— believed there was a vast untapped market for quality American-made products such as ours. Those someones were right.

If you've recently gotten instructions similar to the ones I received back in 1993 with Motorola and in 1994 with Dell Computer, or if you're part of an ongoing enterprise still considering expansion to the Asia-Pacific, this book is for you. Even if you're considering expansion to another foreign land, not the Asia-Pacific, this book is still full of helpful ideas, advice, and shortcuts. Many of the concepts are relevant regardless of your ultimate destination.

What I want to do in these pages is to let you leverage on my experience so you don't have to create an entirely new foundation yourself. There is no need to reinvent the wheel, nor is there a need for you to make mistakes I've already made. Of course, feel free to make your own different mistakes—doing that is more original than repeating mine, and you'll undoubtedly learn from them.

I want to explain, too, my emphasis on the Asia-Pacific as a frontier. It's an apt way to view business start-up in Asia, and it can change your whole perspective, as it has mine, from seeing foreign start-up as chock-full of problems to viewing it as a challenge, from looking in despair at a set of seemingly insurmountable differences to encountering numerous exciting opportunities to discover similarities.

The more you recognize the untapped depths of the Asia-Pacific markets, and the more you see the potential (as yet unrealized) of business partnering in Asia, as well as simple product and service expansion into this market, the easier it is to anticipate the adventure you're embarking upon.

Being an adventurer, no matter what the context, revolves around seeing possibility in every situation, not allowing yourself to be hemmed in by how things have always been done. There is no "always"; this is a new frontier. We've gone to the oceans and plumbed their depths. We've explored space, which some called the final frontier, but I'd dispute that. Creating the reality of a global marketplace is the final frontier. Asian consumers are hungry for quality American products, and Asian corporations are ready to do business with Americans—provided the Americans bring their businesses to Asia with a respect for cultural norms and a knowledge of laws, regulations and standards governing the business of Asian countries.

The catch-phrase in business over the past few years has been "thinking outside of the box," and nowhere is such an approach more useful than in foreign start-up, where "the box" consists of everything that has worked in the United States. If you take the box with you to Asia, it's excess baggage. You'll bring it back unopened, and you'll bring it back much sooner than you had planned. Your surefire, tried-and-true United States business strategies will largely let you down, and your business will almost undoubtedly fail.

The final frontier is one where you can have the adventure of both give and take. And if you do it right, your presence among the pioneers in this frontier will empower and enrich not only you and your corporation but the infrastructure of an entire continent, and the people of that continent, both directly and indirectly. Not bad for a day's work. And that's why I call it an adventure.

If I can save you the trouble of reinvention, enabling you to focus your energies on the adventure and complexities of the start-up, I've done what I set out to do. If I can help you create an Asia-Pacific division that succeeds (when more than 50 percent of overseas American business expansions fail, with an almost 85 percent failure rate in the Asia-Pacific), I've done what I set out to do. If, through you, I can directly or indirectly have an impact on the millions of people American expansion helps, aiding them through contributing to the health of a foreign economy, I've done what I set out to do. If, along the way, I can help you create a bullish Asian market for your product or service, and in the process turn you into a wealthy person, that wouldn't be so bad either, as I'll bet you will agree.

And if I can convey to you something important to me on a personal level—the deep caring and respect I have come to feel for the Asia-Pacific region and its people, and my love of its cultures, customs, and methods of communication—I will have far exceeded my goals for this book.

Many people lead by habit or long experience; a problem arises and they instinctively (or, more often, through hard-won knowledge) know how to handle it, but are hard-pressed to put pen to paper or fingers to keyboard to reproduce the steps involved in problem-solving and solutions. It's like the old adage about art: I don't know why I like it, but I know what I like. You may not know why you handle many business decisions and interactions in certain ways, but you know your approach works in most cases, most of the time, and so you stick with it. And it does work, at least in the United States.

Like anyone might, I started my Asian adventure applying the same skills, same approaches, the same everything to the Asian start-up as I would have any start-up. And while I certainly knew a lot of effort would go into creating and carrying out the expansion plan, I didn't factor in that expansion into the Asia-Pacific (or any foreign country) would mean learning entirely new sets of rules and entirely new ways of doing business.

Think of it as self-expansion: Even as you plan and execute a corporate expansion you engage in a self-expansion of huge proportions because you're starting fresh with what you thought you finished back when you clawed your way out of the mailroom and into the boardroom—you're learning how business works. This time, though, you're learning it in and about a foreign country, with another language (or several), vastly different customs, and, most likely, a totally different approach to doing business.

I remember a Steve Martin comedy routine about traveling, where he'd put on a half-wondering, half-annoyed voice and drawl, "Those foreigners! They have a different word for everything!" Language differences are the first major barrier, but if the differences stopped there, an interpreter would get you past the obstacles. But it's more than just words, which is part of what I want to convey to you. A successful entry into the Asia-Pacific market means recognizing, respecting, and, most essentially, adapting to the market's many unfamiliar cultural, custom, and communication norms in business, whether obvious or hidden. There are some constants about business, but no matter where you go or with whom you do it, every culture "does" business a little or a lot differently. Adapting will mean the difference between success and failure.

For that reason, you will see a recurrent theme about adaptation in this book. I firmly believe it is our job, as guests of a foreign people, to drop the distinctly American entitlement ethos that expects others to adapt to us, no matter whose ground we find ourselves on. While many foreign countries offer bilingual education, resulting in a population that often speaks English, we must not assume that the people of any given country will meet us at our door when we're standing on their front porch.

As a sign of respect, and as an indication of our commitment to and seriousness about partnering in business with other cultures, we must learn to be flexible and adaptive. "When in Rome...", the saying goes, and never is the maxim more true than when our reason for being in Rome—or the Asia-Pacific—is business.

Adventure is about flexibility and adaptation to the unexpected. Your hosts will begin to develop trust and respect for you if you can form a graceful, orderly line to their country's door—and, of course, if you come bearing a product or service of quality and reliability. Whether you find yourself eating fried termites offered to you as a symbol of respect from a high Chinese official, as I did, or standing in a Quonset hut in Manchuria in the dead of night, the temperature registering at 50 degrees below zero, your welcoming committee nowhere to be seen because of a communication glitch, just another challenge in my adventure, the principle is the same: The success or failure of your expansion is largely in your hands. It is up to you to determine not only that you end up with success, but also how you choose to get there.

As we start the new millennium, it is fitting that there is just one frontier left to be explored. Read on, and I believe you will see this as the opportunity and challenge and adventure that it is.

I will add that I have been fortunate, both personally and professionally. And while it's true that I've made a considerable fortune heading a start-up effort in the Asia-Pacific, I'm not talking about money when I talk about what I have received. What I have received is much more difficult to measure. I have been welcomed into a culture I knew little of when I first set foot on Asian soil. There is a grace and a sense of timeless honor in both the land and the people of Asia, and both were extended to me with unfailing and remarkable generosity. I was allowed my mistakes and my sometimes awkward attempts at adapting to a foreign culture. Along the way, I was helped in ways large and small by natives of my host country. Despite being on their turf, sometimes competing with Asian products and services, the competitive nature of the relationships did not overwhelm the generosity and willingness to help. For this I will always be grateful; it has taught me to be more generous, I believe.

That is, perhaps, the other, as yet unspoken, part of why I have written this book: I have received so much, and I want to give back. I want to ease the entry of American businesses into the Asia-Pacific, even while thanking its people by doing my own small part to help make the American corporate presence on Asian soil as much like the native culture as possible: graceful, respectful, and honorable.

Your marching orders are in: Start a division in Asia-Pacific. Better yet, build it and make it work!

And off we go, into the final frontier.

1

Asia Doesn't Exist

Culture, Customs & Creativity in Asia

At night, to a first-time visitor, Hong Kong can look like Manhattan. The skyline is lit up with a thousand different colors, and towering high-rises. Once you travel the 45 minutes between the airport and the city—another dose of exhaustion after the flight—the streets are packed with people hurrying here and there. For a moment, if you don't look around, you can pretend or even believe you're somewhere familiar, a place where you can slip into a deli and order a Reuben, and though the counter-help might be surly, he'll be surly in a way you understand. Any notions you have along these lines are dispelled almost immediately, however, as your eyes encounter unknown symbols on signs and faces that look totally unlike your own. You are frozen in place by the massive throngs of people rushing past and around you as you look in vain for something familiar.

Welcome to Asia! For you, this experience may still lie ahead; for me, the year was 1993, and although I'd traveled quite a bit in other countries, I'd never lived in Asia before. Now here I was on a hot, humid night, exhausted and alone, my family following in a few weeks once I'd gotten us settled into our new home. The rush of emotions I experienced in those first moments in Asia was enough to stop me in my tracks. Landing in Hong Kong was akin to taking a flight from Redwood City, California, the town where I was raised (with a population around fifty thousand when I was growing up), to New York

City, only multiplied by a thousand, maybe two thousand. And like a foreigner landing in the United States for the first time, mistakenly assuming that America contains one people, one ethos, one culture, I believed—at first—that Hong Kong fully represented the continent I was entering. All I was aware of was the daunting task ahead of me, learning one entirely new culture.

As I searched for a sign that might help get me to a cab, I was struck suddenly by the enormity of what I was doing. I had an urgent sense of anxiety, but was also aware of the buzz of adventure, a dawning sense of excitement. I was further outside of my comfort zone than I'd ever been, but beneath the anxiety that the departure and arrival produced, I felt charged by the newness and the difference of what I would be doing in the weeks and months ahead. Had I known that the colors I saw in Hong Kong's night sky were just some of many in the prism that is the Asia-Pacific—fifty countries with fifty cultures and customs and languages that form the illusion outsiders believe to be one entity—I might have turned and run for the plane heading back to the States. As it was, I didn't know, and I'm thankful for that now, because I was standing not at the edge of a precipice but on the cusp of an adventure.

Breathe

Dr. Fritz Perls, an eminent therapist and practitioner in the field of holistic mental health, once said "Fear is only excitement without the breath." I didn't know this then, but instinctively I did know to stop—or, more accurately, remain frozen for a moment—and breathe. It's the first piece of advice I'll give you before we move into the more business related ideas, but it's too simple, and too effective, to put off: Take a deep breath and learn.

In your early days in Asia, you're going to find yourself feeling more helpless, more lost, and more out of control than you're accustomed to. If you're the one tapped to lead the start-up or expansion effort, you are, by definition, a corporate success: You're competent, confident, and on the ball. You're not going to feel comfortable with the mix of feelings that come at you and from you early on in Asia, because you don't tend to feel them on your own turf. This isn't your turf, though, so all bets are off. When you first feel yourself slipping (or crashing) out of your comfort zone, the two most helpful things to do are: Breathe (slowly, intentionally, and with focus) and recognize that we're most creative and most likely to learn when we're out of our comfort zone. Here's the formula:

unfamiliar situations + creative problem-solving = new solutions and learnings.

Once I remembered that I had to breathe (sure, it sounds simple, but try finding a cab if you're not breathing!), I got myself unfrozen from the middle of the concourse. I then began to learn some key lessons that I want to pass on to you, lessons that will help you with the practical aspects of your first experience in Asia. Some of the lessons were things I employed that worked; others I didn't know to employ, which meant I learned the hard way. Whichever the case, they have a common bond: They will help you let go of the worry and anxiety such a huge change can present, and shift your focus instead to the adventure, the challenge, and the excitement. And when you're the pioneer in the final frontier, you need your energy to be focused and working for you.

Each of the suggestions I'll share with you comes from a perspective that I've developed over the past six years in Asia, a perspective I want you to know up front. I alluded to it earlier, telling you about my first moments in Hong Kong, but let me elaborate on my image of Asia-Pacific as viewed through a prism.

Finally you're ready to enter a culture in which the Final Four has nothing to do with the NCAA Championships. Instead, the Final Four are the four foundations—respect, authority and obedience, honor and keeping agreements, and trust—upon which Asian cultures are built, and learning to operate in ways consistent with these cultural values will mean the difference between success and failure. In this chapter I will talk about the philosophical and moral foundations of each of these areas, and give you specific examples and approaches to use when doing business in Asia-Pacific, things I've learned from my own adventures.

Prepare Ahead of Time

We already know you're probably not from Asia, since that's a basic assumption underlying the ideas contained in this book. For now, let's say you're an American. With that assumption made, you know that America is the proverbial melting pot, made up of people of different ethnic, religious, political, and cultural backgrounds.

We're all bonded, though, by one essential common connection: We share a language. While there are fifty states in the Union, and while people of different ethnic backgrounds may speak various languages at home, English is the dominant language. More than anything else, a language defines a country, either connecting it or separating it from other countries.

Bridges are made, of course, across languages, but we generally feel most at home, most surrounded by the familiar, when we are on our own soil or on soil where the language is shared, even if an accent creates some differences. So, for instance, the American traveling in Great Britain is likely to feel less culture shock than the American traveling in Russia or Japan or any other country where the primary language is not English.

Now enter Asia into the equation. To the average American, Asia is a country. It's actually a continent, of course, but to the typical American, Asia can be defined by a set of commonly held perceptions, such as the following:

- *Asians speak Chinese or Japanese*
- *Asia is primarily urban, with overcrowded cities*
- *Asians are more respectful than Americans of their elders and superiors*
- *Asian government is more autocratic than American government*
- *Asian families are limited in the number of children they may have*

I could go on with the list of what your typical American believes to be true about Asia and Asians and then discuss each statement as true or false, but the point I most want to make here is less related to stereotypes—which I'll deal with later—and more related to the title of this chapter: "Asia Doesn't Exist."

There is no such thing as "Asia" if you're defining it as a single entity, something with one language, one culture, one food, one people, one anything. Asia consists of fifty countries and territories, and that means multiple languages—and even more dialects. It also means multiple cultures, sets of customs, and ways of doing business. I bring this up now because it is the foundation upon which any further advice rests. If you follow my suggestions but still believe you will be dealing with a single entity, your start-up efforts will not succeed. You may succeed in China, let's say, where you've done your research and followed my advice, but you're going to be hopelessly lost in Japan, where the preparations you made for China have little or no relevance.

What you have to do is take each piece of advice I give you, with the exception of breathing (you can do that anywhere, and I hope you will), and apply it specifically to the Asia-Pacific country and culture you're in. This is a bit tricky because, in a sense, what I'm saying is that you don't want to generalize even as I give you a set of generalizations to consider. Here's how it works: In general terms, you can safely assume that the first-time traveler to Asia will feel overwhelmed on occasion, given the different languages, cultures, and customs. What I don't want you to do is take that generalization and assume that you will feel *equally* overwhelmed in each country or territory, or that the customs in *each* region will be equally foreign or inexplicable to you.

I want you to generalize the knowledge that you should be prepared for differences, and then I want you to remain open-minded, willing to watch and listen and learn in each specific region, some of which will be easier to adapt to than others. It won't work to generalize in certain cases; for instance, Japan is not China and China is not Malaysia when it comes to specific ways in which the government supports foreign enterprise. What *can* be generalized is that Japan and China and Malaysia and every other country and territory will be different from what you are accustomed to.

Remember the caveat to that message you got from corporate, the message to start an Asian division? The caveat was "Build it and make it work." You're at a critical juncture in terms of making it work when you reach the point where you prepare yourself for cultural differences, so take care, recognize that you've got lots of learning ahead of you, and whatever else you do, don't forget: Asia doesn't exist.

You must approach your expansion as if you are expanding into fifty different countries simultaneously if you're intending to expand into all of Asia. You're probably not (and if you are, I hope you'll reconsider, as we'll discuss later when we talk about foreign start-up and risk-taking behaviors). What you're probably doing is planning to expand into one country first, adding others down the line, or a few countries to begin with. One of the biggest mistakes I've seen, however, is assuming that because several countries are in Asia, they are all subject to the same approach. Bad move.

Having said that, here's what I learned in my earliest days and weeks in the Asia that doesn't exist.

Language

Any number of foreign-language tapes or books can help you to prepare for your entry into a new country. Learning a new language can be a daunting task, but if you break down your stay into categories, it will lessen the overwhelming nature of language acquisition. Here's how I wish I'd categorized language then, and how I've done it since. First learn the words you will need on arrival in the foreign country. Here's a list of the words I've found most useful:

Airport/Arrival:

Cab/Taxi	Restroom	Money	Translator
Airplane	Food	Exchange	Baggage Claim
Arrival	Drink	Subway	Rental Car
Departure	Hotel	Bus	Airport Paging
Telephone	Police/Security	Shuttle	Delay/Delayed

Hotel:

Room	Nonsmoking	Laundry
Reservation	Smoking	Room Number
Room Service	Concierge	Luggage
Restaurant	Fax	Exercise Room/Gym

General Words/Terms:

Police	Is there a…	Left
Do you know where…	How much…	Right
How do I…	When is…	Straight

You'll want to add your own key words, of course, but this is a solid starting list for the situations in which you'll first find yourself. It helps to separate the "over" and the "whelming." Though it's not a word, imagine something as simply being "whelming," or a whole lot to deal with. But when you add the "over," you're letting something get bigger than you are. Language acquisition can feel overwhelming, no doubt about it, unless you're one of the lucky people who picks up languages at the drop of a hat (I'm not). So, try to break it down ad see it as predictably hard instead of unpredictably impossible.

The First Moments

So, there I was in Hong Kong, and no one had told me that Asia doesn't exist; I was totally unaware of the fact that fifty different countries were reflected in the faces of the people rushing around me. All I knew was that I had just entered one unfamiliar country, and that seemed complicated enough. Because I'm a problem-solver, like you, I found a cab—and spent the entire breakneck cab ride worrying myself over whether I was heading toward one of those worst-nightmare kinds of hotels you sometimes find.

I'm not a worrier by nature, but the unfamiliarity of my surroundings found me being lots of things I'm usually not, including a worrier, a helpless-lost-soul, and an anxiety-ridden businessman who was suddenly nearly overcome with hunger for a Dunkin Donut or some other caloric symbol of everything I'd ever known.

At the end of the cab ride, there was the hotel—the Grand Hyatt, complete with a three-story marble atrium and an English-speaking desk staff. The contrast between my worries and the reality leads me to my second piece of advice: Don't let your expectations rule you.

As soon as I walked into the Grand Hyatt, my anxiety lifted and a strong sense of excitement started to take over. Maybe this wasn't going to be so bad after all. Time and again, traveling and doing business in

Asia-Pacific, I've learned and relearned the same lesson: Expectations based on nothing get in the way.

In your early days in Asia, you have nothing upon which to base your expectations except what you've heard from others along the way. What others say can be helpful, and also highly suspect. I'm not the fairest judge when I've just spent twenty-four hours crossing continents on an airplane, and maybe you're not either. I'm not wild about the unfamiliar at first, and maybe you're not either. Remember that often the viewpoints you get about specifics like hotels and generalities like continents are going to come from folks who have just wrapped up a twenty-four-hour flight after a tour of duty in a country that made them face things they'd never faced before and brought out feelings of helplessness they'd never felt before. Take it all with a huge grain of salt.

Whatever angle you come at this adventure from, one of the most important things you can remember is that each experience is going to be completely new for you, and layering it with all sorts of preconceived notions and expectations will just slow you down. Instead of worrying needlessly and fruitlessly, why not use the cab ride to the hotel to some of these things:

- *think about how you're going to spend the next day,*
- *close your eyes for a power nap,*
- *try for a tip from the driver on where to find the best food in town,*
- *look out the window and take in all of the rich new sights*

I didn't see a thing that first night in Hong Kong because I was far too occupied with anxious thoughts. Let it go if it's out of your control. And if it's in your control, you shouldn't be worrying about it to begin with; you should be focusing on a specific game plan for how you're going to handle whatever "it" is. Letting go of expectations is simple when you get right down to it, but it requires something from you: a willingness to recognize that you can either go with the flow, or let it take you under.

Mixed Feelings

Speaking of taking you under, let me give you another piece of advice related to sanity and emotion. If you're like me, you don't spend a lot of time thinking about how you feel. It's not exactly the norm in the corporate culture. I don't know about your company, but at Dell, we didn't often walk down the corridors saying, "Hey, Phil, I was wondering, you've seemed kind of down lately, kind of emotionally fragile. Want to talk about it?" It would probably be a better world if there was more of that, but then, I imagine many of us would avoid the corridors. Since it's probably not like that where you work either, and since you may not be accustomed to dealing with unfamiliar feelings (or, for that matter, familiar feelings), my next piece of advice is important, even if it strikes you as out of place in a business book. It's precisely because this situation is out of place in the corporate world that I'm including it, because it's not the kind of thing you're accustomed to, and it's not the kind of thing business books are going to mention: Be ready for the full range of emotions.

I told you how I felt that first evening in Hong Kong, and confessed that I wasn't used to having those feelings. Neither are you, at least not in your conscious, "out there" persona, right? Any anxiety or helplessness or feeling-lost you do, you probably do in the privacy of your own head. Here's the problem: Making a move into a foreign culture (and then multiplying that by fifty) is going to make it damn near impossible for you to continue the charade.

I remember when we were expecting our first child. My then wife was a strong woman, and she's one of those people who seems to have a strong pain threshold, and she kind of laughed off the notion of pain when it came up in our childbirth classes. We both did, because we knew that she'd breathe right through the labor and delivery. Pain just didn't get to her the same way it gets to some people. And then the labor started, and sure enough, she was breezing along and we were congratulating each other on how tough she was…it wasn't easy, but she was coping. Then we got to the hospital and found out she was in really early labor. That was disheartening, since she'd used up so much energy "breezing" through the easy part! Later she told me that she'd never experienced anything like that pain. She said it was beyond anything she could imagine; the emotions were so intense, so overwhelming, so constant, and so unfamiliar that she lost all ability to cope. She wasn't prepared at all. The whole thing, she said, made her feel crazy; it changed her entire way of viewing pain and her coping skills and ability.

Not to make light of her experience, because the two can't be compared on some levels, but I see some similarities here: If you're not prepared for the enormity of the undertaking, the unfamiliarity of what you're about to do, it is going to be much more difficult for you. If you approach the change with a cavalier attitude, assuming that your old ways of coping will suffice, your reliable problem-solving methods and ways of looking at the world, you're in for trouble.

Moving yourself, your business and, if applicable, your family to a foreign country is a far bigger deal than you can begin to imagine. The feelings that will confront you, and the fact that you are the one responsible for the success or failure of this venture, as well as the fact that your family will likely hold you accountable for their own anxiety and distress at a time when you may already be overwhelmed both emotionally and professionally can challenge your sanity. One of the best ways to cope with the challenge is to prepare for it, to recognize in advance that this isn't going to be like anything you've been through before. If you over prepare and it's easier than you expected, that's a bonus. If you under prepare and get hit by emotional chaos, both your own and that of all the people depending on you, that's far worse: That lack of preparation readies the soil for the seeds of what is going to ultimately grow into the failure of the start-up. I guarantee it.

The Final Four

If being prepared for the possible emotional onslaught is important—and it is—so is the next point I want to make, and it's equally related to the complexity of doing business in a prism made up of many languages, many cultures, and many approaches to business.

You're a success in your field or you wouldn't be leading the start-up effort, and so you've developed all sorts of approaches to problem-solving, idea-creation, and product or service delivery. Some of your approaches haven't worked; you've thrown those out and learned from the effort. Others have worked, with wild success or with more moderate, steadier reliability, and you've tweaked things here and adjusted things there and you've got a good, stable gig going with those widgets. And so the boss—maybe that's you—gets an idea one day over takeout *kung pao* chicken, and next thing you know you're in a jet soaring thirty thousand feet over an ocean, wondering where you'd be if your boss had chosen lobster, say, for lunch that day. And, of course, you're also probably wondering what possessed you to agree to do this.

Here's what possessed you: You're an entrepreneur at heart, someone who loves the risk, the challenge, the excitement of starting something new. You're an execution person, the one who always gets the job done. If you say it will happen, it happens. Sound like you?

Over the years, you've honed your abilities and gotten into a routine with the way you get things done. Up here in the air on your way to Asia, you're nervous, sure, but you also have a solid number of successful years under your belt, and so any nervousness you have isn't about whether you can cut it professionally; it's more about how the family will take the move, or whether you'll hate not being able to get great buffalo wings, things like that.

You're so confident in your abilities, your tried-and-true methods, that it never occurs to you to worry about how it will go the first time you sit down to do business with Asian partners. At least, that's pretty much how it went for me. Try this scenario: You're sitting in a small hotel room that has been converted to a meeting suite. Your Asian partners, all from Malaysia, are seated in a semicircle. There is no table; you don't like this because it makes note-taking awkward, but they didn't provide a table, and you don't want to criticize their meeting style right now since you're sure this is the one where you're going to get the big commitment, the signatures on the dotted line. Things are going well; the talk seems jovial and upbeat—not with the backslapping you might find at an American meeting, but you've already learned to expect a more reserved approach over here. As the leader of the Asian delegation speaks, leading up to the agreement, you turn toward him and cross your legs so you can rest your legal pad on one knee; you want to write down something he's saying. You look up from the paper when he suddenly stops talking midsentence, and you see that every person in the room has blanched, their expressions shocked and—is this possible?—angry. You put both feet on the floor and lean forward, intending to ask what's wrong, and you hear a palpable sigh of relief go through the room. The meeting resumes, but something has shifted, and it ends quickly, with the Asian delegation telling you they'll be in touch. You don't know why you're so sure of this, but you're certain they won't.

Respect

In Malaysia, crossing one's legs with the sole of the foot facing another person is considered the height of insults. It is rude, offensive, far beyond boorish behavior. It is a deal breaker. I was very, very fortunate when I was the one who did this in a meeting much like the one I just described because I was taken aside later by a member of the delegation and informed of my mistake, and the deal, fortunately, was made in the end. But I lost two months in the meantime, repairing damaged relationships.

You may think this is absurd. Don't they know you're an American, and not aware of every nonverbal nuance of a foreign language? Don't they understand that if you wanted to insult them, you'd do it by not doing business with them, or by showing up late for every meeting, or by talking when they talk, or by any of a host of different American methods for communicating disrespect?

The answer is simple: no. Reverse the situation and you'll see what I mean. Imagine you and your team meeting with someone from another culture who wants to do business with your company. Things are going well, and then, out of the blue, this person holds up his hand with the middle finger extended…and he just sits like that, giving you the finger. What would your first reaction be? Disbelief? Irritation? Even once you understood that he didn't realize it was an insult, you might well be heard to grumble, "Well, if he's going to do business with Americans, he ought to learn what it means when he does things like that."

We're not in Kansas anymore, Toto. It's your job to adapt to your host culture, not their job to adapt to yours. You want to do business with them—that's how this whole thing started, right? It's presumptuous to expect your host to do all of the adapting and interpreting.

Keep in mind my experience as you read this next piece of advice, which embellishes the "When in Rome" adage. You are on foreign soil, with foreign customs, and you have a dual task.

First, you must familiarize yourself with these customs. A number of excellent books deal with this topic, so I'm not going to reinvent the wheel. A simple Internet search or traditional library search will yield all the reading you can do on this for years to come. The second thing you must do, at all times and with good grace, isn't mentioned enough in the business and culture books I've read.

Because Asia now has a more established history of doing business with both Westerners and with persons from other parts of the world, business practices are not as cut-and-dried as they once were. In the past, it might have been easier to simply identify the "Asian approach" to doing business, but this just doesn't remain static. Many Asia businesses, and businesspersons, have Westernized their business practices; for instance, you might observe that a sales team wants to get to the point rather than spending quite as much time on relationship-building, which has long been an Asian hallmark in business. You might notice that ceremony takes on less importance in another business setting. The best way to approach customs and business practices is to observe— watch for what is done and how it is done, and for what seems to be the culture within any given business—and be open-minded and never assume a certain approach will be employed. Ask your Asian partners when they would like to go over numbers; ask if they would like to have dinner first. In other words: Be flexible.

One of the things I've noticed about myself during my time in Asia is that I've become much more flexible. Maybe part of it is just a maturational process, part of the process of layering on the years and the experiences and the realization that you can't always get what you want. Some of it, though, is related directly to my experience in Asia-Pacific, where I have learned, often the hard way, that resistance is futile. Here's what I mean:

I travel a great deal within Asia, and although the flights are generally fine and the service great, one thing I still struggle with is a bureaucratic clinging to the rules—whether they make sense or not—that nearly drives me crazy at times. I was in the Beijing airport once, running late for my flight, and there was a long line in emigration. Off to the side was a sign that said "If Your Plane Is Departing in Less Than 15 Minutes, Use This Line." Under this sign was a marker board that got updated frequently, and it had a few flights listed on it—but not mine. A guard stood at the board, guarding the line and occasionally erasing and adding flight numbers. My plane was leaving in fourteen minutes, so I left the long line, knowing, from the sign, that I should be able to go through the shorter line. The guard looked at my flight information, looked at his board, looked at his watch...and shook his head.

I asked why, and he just pointed toward the long line and shook his head again. After spending about three frustrating minutes in the long, unmoving line, it was obvious I'd miss my flight unless I went through the short line, so I tried again, showing the guard all the papers, my watch, the clock on the wall, anything I could think of. He slowly looked at his marker board again—my flight number still wasn't there— and shook his head. It would be hours before the next flight, and I'd miss a critical meeting if I didn't make this one. Now we were down to six, maybe seven minutes. I started wondering what the legal rules are for justifiable homicide in Beijing, but just then, the guard, with painstaking care, erased a few numbers from his board, and slowly, slowly, wrote my flight number. I sprinted for the line, raced through it, and made my flight with about thirty seconds to spare. As I ran down the carpeted hall to the airplane, the guard's expression was in my mind; he smiled and shrugged in a universal sign of regret and helplessness.

Settled in my seat, able to be a little more charitable, I was suddenly aware that the guard had absolutely no latitude to do anything other than what he had been told to do. He was not to let passengers through his line until their flight number was given to him to mark on the board. And he didn't. I had no control, which obviously fed my stress, but what I failed to recognize and accept was that neither did he. I was railing against reality, fighting something that was not going to change, and making it worse in the meantime.

You see what I mean, no doubt. When we're most stressed, we're also probably most likely to get rigid, insisting on exerting control. The problem with this is that the reason we're most stressed to begin with, typically, is that we're aware that we don't have control. The more control you try to exert, the more aware you become that you are only one small piece of the puzzle, and that the other pieces are often hidden or incomprehensible to you since they're not culturally familiar. It's a vicious and destructive cycle; you feel out of control, so you try to exert control. That makes you feel more out of control, so you...well, you get the picture. Here's how I visualize it in a technical business paradigm:

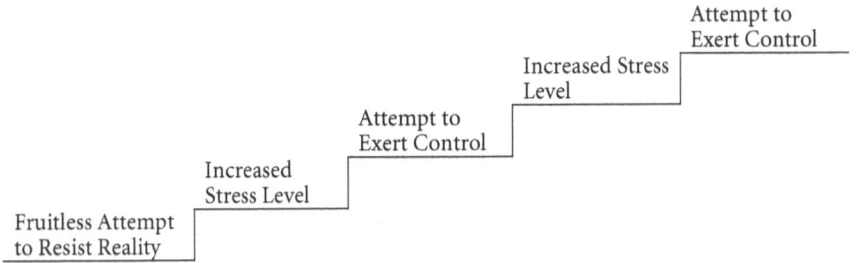

The obvious question: What's wrong with this picture? The obvious answer is a question, too: Who is running operations while you're chasing your tail around in circles? You can apply my model to any business situation or, for that matter, any personal situation in which reality exists in a form you don't want to accept. This is not to suggest you should throw your hands into the air in every situation, of course; you know from experience that you actually have a great deal of sway in the universe.

However, when you enter a foreign country and face day after day of languages, cultures, customs, and ways of doing business unfamiliar to you, you have three choices:

Rail at Reality—Spend your time complaining about the bizarre local customs and comparing Asian culture unfavorably to American culture.

Resist Reality—Don't just rail about it, spend your energy fighting it, arguing against it, and trying to change customs that sometimes have a history spanning hundreds of years (good luck!).

Respect Reality—Accept that what is, is, and that your energy needs to go toward your start-up right now, not toward tilting at windmills.

What it all comes down to is that you're being flexible when you respect reality. You're going with the flow, taking things as they come. You're going to be plenty busy in this foreign country trying to familiarize yourself with an entirely different way of doing things, and you're going to be plenty busy in your new job, starting a business in an unfamiliar environment. Don't set yourself up for stress, sanity challenges, and sleepless nights by fighting what cannot (or should not) be changed—not by an American, anyway.

Another note on being flexible. When I described it above as "respecting reality," I chose the word respect for a significant reason. In Asian countries, respect is a big deal. It was one of the things I came to love most about being in Asia: The value structure that is generally in place across the borders within the continent is substantial, and steeped in thousands of years of history and practice.

In most Asian countries, everything is about relationship, much more so than in the United States. Relationships can be divided into three categories—family, friendships, and the work world—and they are generally lifelong. Generations of families live together, school chums are friends from the moment they first enter the schoolhouse doors, and work relationships are extremely important. The fabric of Asia-Pacific is woven of relationships.

If you are to succeed in Asia-Pacific, you must respect the reality of the importance of relationships, which includes the issues of trust and respect for and within relationships. You will see that a group of Japanese investors, for instance, might spend six months getting to know you before they are ever willing to discuss business. They will expect for you to honor them at banquets, at smaller dinners as the trust builds, at all manner of social events where you can be observed and where relationships can begin a natural formation. If you try to "take a meeting" with this group of investors early on, your internal cash register clicking and whirring and ringing (time is money, after all) as time passes without a deal, you will create a sense of distrust and discomfort that is unlikely to be bridged. You will, in other words, have disrespected the most basic of tenets of doing business in the Asia-Pacific market. The result? Take relationship-building seriously, friend, or you will blow your chances right out of the water.

In Asia-Pacific, many rules and customs cannot be ignored, and success requires you to be flexible in many areas. The area that is perhaps most foreign, however, and simultaneously most critical, is the one I want to give you some background and pointers on: It's what I call the Relationship Rule. It may be a "soft science," something that seems hard to quantify, all that immeasurable psychological stuff…but I've seen masters at finance who are completely unskilled in human relations wreck a deal faster than you can say "touchy-feely."

The Relationship Rule

I'm going to assume, since you're reading this, that you want to start or expand your business in Asia. I'm going to further assume that you want that start-up or expansion to be wildly successful, making your company a household name in the Asian markets, bringing untold wealth to investors, and making you rich along the way. Maybe you'll settle for less, but why not start with those assumptions, since they're your secret if not spoken wishes? Okay. So that's where we start, with you in Hong Kong, say, cab found and hotel nicer than you could have imagined. Let's say you're even past jet lag. You're ready to start.

Your laptop is full of statistics and a Power Point presentation that's going to knock the socks off the Asians with whom you want to partner. You've got samples of the product for each potential investor: The widgets, showcased in fancy little black-chrome boxes, look so good even you want one, and you've seen enough widgets to last a lifetime.

Because you have a great marketing and public relations team, you've also brought each investor what our head of marketing calls a "care package." It's a basket full of Made-in-America products, things that are hard to come by over here. It's a soften-them-up collection, something to show that corporate wants to do business and is thinking of the investors.

A meeting has been scheduled for 6 P.M. on your second night in Hong Kong. You'd have preferred the first day, but they didn't seem open to that, so you were flexible and now it's almost meeting time. It's an odd time for the meeting, but they want to meet over food and drinks and you figure, "When in Rome," so that's what you do.

You manage to get through the meeting without making any huge cultural faux pas, a relief. You were a bit worried about that. You present the widgets and you present the baskets, and everyone seems honored by the gesture and appreciative of the thoughtfulness. Things are going well, and as coffee is served, you stand up and make a brief speech thanking your hosts for their time and generosity; the speech, which you've carefully prepared, also seems to go over well. Flipping open your laptop, you click a few buttons, not noticing that the investors all look puzzled, and you launch into your presentation.

Let's look at this situation and discuss three relationship truisms I've become familiar with in my time in Asia. Let my experience serve as both a warning and a guide for you in your own business dealings in Asian countries and cultures.

Relationship Truism No. 1
Strong bonding will not occur in a race against time

Just as there are monetary conversion rates, there is a time conversion rate. It's unspoken; you won't find it posted in a bank or below any clock, but time is handled differently in Asia-Pacific, and this is nowhere more evident than in the world of business development. You are not trying to beat the clock when it comes to forming a bond with your potential Asian business partners. While the "time is money" approach is likely to be a part of your modus operandi, since it is ingrained in American philosophy, it may not sit well in Asia. It may, in fact, feel insulting, as if you simply want to get in, get done, and get out.

When you open your laptop and start in on your pitch right off the bat, you break one of the most basic rules of Asian time conversion. If I was one of your investors and saw it coming, I'd have wanted to warn you, but it would be too late.

In the world of Asian business, and this certainly extends to the merged world of Asian and American businesses, you do not rush into partnerships. You do not pitch a group of Asian businesspersons, no matter how friendly and receptive they are to the shared venture, until you have been given a clear go-ahead by them.

This go-ahead will, at times, seem painfully slow in coming. Do not assume this is because of reservations on the part of the Asians with whom you are doing business. It is not. It is because in Asia-Pacific, the relationship comes first and foremost. Until a relationship has formed between the entities engaged in business, no business will take place. This relationship formation stage can vary in length.

In my first foray into Asia-Pacific, it was a full six months before we began talking business in earnest. We met, got to know each other, shared meals, discussed philosophy and cultural differences, and the like. To me, it more closely resembled the early stages of the formation of friendships, where you get to know someone's likes and dislikes, gauge his or her reactions to you, see how well you get along, and decide whether you want to remain in a relationship together.

There's a good reason for this, and it relates to something I mentioned earlier, which is the permanent nature of relationships in Asia. In a culture in which relationships typically last a lifetime, it makes sense that a long "study period," if you will, is applied before the bond is cemented. To rush into a permanent relationship is foolhardy, since doing so leaves you open to numerous surprises, potentially unpleasant. Instead, with a substantial period of acquaintance, one can be relatively certain that the partnership is advisable.

A word of caution—and I've found this to apply equally to cross-cultural and same- culture business partnerships. If a deal seems to be moving along quickly, with your Asian partner giving you the impression that she or he is eager and in a hurry to get the deal signed, your first reaction may be to think that you've stumbled upon a Westernized Asian business, and one that will be prompt, efficient, and hard-charging—one that is almost too good to be true. But like most things that are too good to be true, it probably is. I have seen many, many joint ventures in China fail for this very reason. The Western partner did not spend the necessary time getting to know the Asian partner, and the Asian partner wanted to get connected with a Western business as soon as possible for any number of reasons. It might be that the Asian partner needs the capital; it might be that the Asian partner is seeking the international strength in a cross-cultural partnership. The point is, it did not matter so much who the Western partner was, simply that there was a Western partner. Like a marriage when someone is simply ready to settle down as opposed to marriage because the partnership is right and appears to have what it will take to sustain it, this kind of hasty pairing is done for all the wrong reasons—and that often becomes painfully apparent down the road.

The more gradual approach, of course, is quite different from how business partnerships are conducted in the United States. For one thing, over the past fifteen or twenty years, mergers have, as often as not, been adversarial, with hostile takeovers occurring with disturbing frequency. Obviously, these types of partnerships are hardly concerned with relationship stability or quality.

However, even when the merger is friendly and mutually beneficial, it is just generally not the American style to devote enough time, energy, and resources to determining whether the partners have shared business philosophies, value systems, and corporate goals.

In my opinion, this is a shame. I believe that the American corporate world would do well to emulate the Asian approach to business partnering. While I was initially often frustrated by the painstaking process that had to occur before making any significant deals, I have come to admire and respect this gradual approach. I have observed firsthand how this process lends stability to new businesses or expansion efforts that might otherwise be even more subject to the tremors and variations in market conditions. A united front—a strong and stable partnership of local expertise and foreign product expertise—can be a powerful force in a market.

The reality, however, is that American business does not generally emulate this relationship philosophy. What this means is that you, as an American doing business in Asia-Pacific, need to make a substantial shift when you embark on your start-up efforts. Your natural inclination may be to head into initial meetings prepared for a pitch, since that's the approach here in the United States. After all, time is money, and in the United States you're going to be judged negatively if you take too long to get to the point.

We are a culture that likes to get to the point. However, in Asia you must be willing to recognize that while preparation is great, and necessary, you won't likely need those charts and graphs for a while. In your initial meetings with Asian partners, your personality, authentic charm, friendliness, and manners are going to be more useful than your laptop computer.

Relationship Truism No. 2
Lack of commitment does not equal disinterest

You'll likely interpret any delay of a move toward delivering your pitch or any delay in response to your pitch as indicating disinterest, as I mentioned earlier, but in Asia-Pacific, focusing on business too quickly or allowing yourself to become discouraged by the Asian lack of commitment early on will damage your efforts. Remind yourself that you are forming a long-term relationship, one that you and your potential Asian partners want to last a lifetime, and it may be easier for you to make this shift. Flexibility is the rule here, as it always is in relationship formation. Follow the lead of your Asian partners and hosts, and recognize that one day in the United States could easily equal three months in Asia.

Relationship Truism No. 3
Asia is founded on respect for authority

You probably already have a sense of the fact that Asian culture is founded on a tradition of clear hierarchy within families and within the workplace. While rooted in many thousands of years of tradition, this foundation has been shaken somewhat by the influx of Westerners to Asian countries, as well as the return of many Asian natives after education or employment in the West, where autocratic or authoritarian hierarchies have lost the strength and power they once held. Despite this, however, the culture—and the business world in particular—is still firmly grounded in an authoritarian and hierarchical structure that emphasizes and rewards respect.

I have already discussed the issue of respect in some detail, but I want to emphasize its importance, particularly as it relates to the hierarchical structure of business relationships and interactions. We are a casual society here in the United States, with a First Amendment approach underlying all of our interactions, whether they occur in the context of interpersonal or business relationships. Americans are raised to believe, to a greater or lesser extent, that our right to speak our minds, our right to challenge authority, is unalienable.

That approach doesn't go over well in just about any context or corner of Asia. The tradition of authority and hierarchy is strong, despite a Western influence, and Americans coming into Asia will be particularly suspect if they challenge authority, especially in front of others, given the disrespect that would signal in Asia.

The best piece of advice I can give you on the "respect" front is to try to imagine how things used to be here in the United States, when respect for elders, whether elders in years or in terms of authority, was tantamount. Imagine it, and then imitate it. And, of course, don't just imagine it, since you'll have many clear examples of how it's done:

Watch how Asian natives interact with one another to help you to identify the patterns of interaction, the ways in which respect is communicated in the Asian cultures.

Authority and Obedience

At times, the line drawn between obedience and respect is quite fine. The way I tend to view it is that obedience is operationalized respect. Respect is the concept and obedience is the action. When your boss asks you to do something, it may be phrased as a request, but everyone knows it's not; it's an instruction, and you generally follow it unless there's some good reason not to—a reason you've discussed and come to an agreement on with your boss. This is obedience, but there's a branching off here between American and Asian cultures, since in Asia-Pacific you're much less likely to have that kind of discussion with your boss. The underlying assumption in Asia is that your boss is your boss because she or he knows what's what and doesn't need you to interfere in the decision-making process.

There is **one major exception to this rule**, however, and that's in the area of quality circles, a practice that has its root in Asian corporate culture and was later adopted in many American businesses. In the quality circle, employees of all ranks work together in teams to brainstorm and problem-solve; the ideas and solutions generated in quality circles are then passed on to management. However, even with quality circles, final authority rests in the hands of upper management, and the circles are not and were never intended to replace the hierarchical structure in business.

One of the primary reasons quality circles were created was to better generate practical solutions to frontline problems.

With or without the quality-circle structure, Asians consider following orders part of the respect for authority, the honoring of the hierarchical structure that exists in the corporate environment (and throughout Asian society in general). While you'll be partnering with Asian natives, and thus not often in a position, perhaps, to give or take orders, the area in which obedience is most likely to be an issue is in your dealings with your own staff in front of Asian partners.

Because it might be the norm in your company for there to be a give and take of ideas, a practice that may appear as a challenge to your authority to someone unfamiliar with the less hierarchical and less formalized practices of American business, you must exercise care in this area.

Given the less formalized structure in our corporate world, your employees might well challenge something you say in front of your Asian partners. If it's the norm in your company and/or in your personal leadership style, these challenges won't bother you; it might not occur to you to be concerned about how it appears. However, the observation of this interchange by the Asian partners may serve to undercut your authority and the seeming stability and strength of your company. An Asian might see this challenge and interpret it as an indication of your weak leadership or the instability and/or insubordination of your staff. Keep in mind, of course, that the interpretations will vary based on how traditional the firm is that is doing the interpreting.

To you then, the member of the less traditional corporate culture, colleagues throwing ideas around or an employee acting as devil's advocate is no big deal. In fact, in American business, such a role is generally seen as productive. To the more traditional of your Asian partners (and this traditional approach will still be the rule rather than the exception, even as this continues to change as a result of exposure to Western business culture), the perception and interpretation may go more like this:

> **Perception No. 1:** You propose an idea regarding transportation of widget components from rural production facilities to the main factory on the outskirts of Hong Kong
>
> **Interpretation No. 1:** You are the leader of the start-up team, proposing plans and solutions as any good leader does, and your employees are listening to you respectfully, indicating

that your team is well run and respects authority and the existing hierarchy.

Perception No. 2: Your production manager shakes her head and says it won't work; the widget parts are notoriously fragile before they're placed in the protective covering lining the widget, and many will be damaged on the trip into Hong Kong

Interpretation No. 2: You have just lost control of your team. Your production manager is rude, shaking her head as you speak (a form of interruption, since it focuses attention off of you and onto her, and since it also clearly indicates that she disagrees with what you are saying). In addition, assuming your employee is correct, you have just "lost face," since you should have known that the widget components are fragile; it shouldn't be necessary for your subordinate to tell you this. By disagreeing with you in front of the potential partners, and by showing that her knowledge is superior to yours, your team has embarrassed the Asian partners and raised questions about both your leadership and your competence.

Perception No. 3: You appear annoyed, although it's nothing personal; you're just annoyed at the situation, and you instantly agree that your production manager is correct and ask her if she has an alternative suggestion.

Interpretation No. 3: You have just underscored the impressions created when your subordinate disagreed with you. While subordinate/superior distinctions are not always so pronounced in the United States, in Asia-Pacific the hierarchy is closely observed as an indication of the strength and stability of a corporation, as well as the leadership and competence of its employees, regardless of rank. You have further added to the negative interpretation by your expression of annoyance, as feelings are typically closely guarded in Asian cultures. For instance, polite behavior rather than obvious irritation would dictate an impassive response to most situations. By acknowledging your lack of knowledge, you have also underscored your employee's superior knowledge in this area, and that raises questions about competence, which in turn results in loss of face. (We'll get to a more detailed discussion of the importance of "face" in Asian cultures in a moment.)

Perception No. 4: Your employee suggests combining two of the rural facilities so that the widget components and the protective coating are manufactured in the same plant, thus eliminating the traveling problem. You agree and move on.

Interpretation No. 4: Again, the impression of your employee being better informed than you is reinforced. You have chosen your employees poorly, picking people who don't have the proper respect for authority; therefore, perhaps you don't know what you're doing.

For the reasons shown above, it is essential that you discuss this issue openly with your staff. You must educate them about the Asian cultural norm regarding obedience and make it clear that you are not shifting your overall approach to authority or the free exchange of ideas, but are instead being flexible and responsive to Asian tradition, and protecting your company's image in the process. As such, it will be important for your staff to save challenges for moments when they are unobserved by those outside of your company.

Honor and Keeping Agreements

A corollary to the issue of respect is that honor is of supreme importance in Asian countries. In the United States, it would be unthinkable for the Secretary of the Treasury to resign if there was a major fluctuation in the stock market (we've had numerous fluctuations in the late 90's, as you doubtless know, and Robert Rubin, the previous Secretary, resigned when he was good and ready, and it wasn't because of shame to the best of my knowledge. In Asia, though, this would be a normal and even expected response. We do not take this same approach to honor in business in the United States, and so Americans doing business in Asia-Pacific often find it unfathomable when actions are dictated by the concept of honor. This is not to suggest, of course, that Americans are not honorable in business; we simply communicate our honor differently. We do not have the age-old tradition regarding "face" so prevalent in Asia.

Trust

Trust also plays a pivotal role within the Asian workplace and in partnerships between Asians and Americans. I view it as the natural outgrowth that results when attention is paid to respect, obedience, and honor. When these factors are not treated with the gravity they require, the obvious natural outgrowth is distrust, and the effect on business partnerships can be devastating.

Think, for a moment, about your own workplace, independent of any relationships or dealings you're having with Asian partners. If your workplace is like most, there are smooth periods and then rocky phases, perhaps times when the company is going through growing pains or is experiencing some sort of instability that results in an overall sense of instability amongst employees. What it all comes down to is trust—an employee's sense that she or he can trust the organization to be and do as expected, and an organizational sense that employees can be trusted to be and do as expected. In the ideal corporate world, these issues would never arise; both individually and collectively, organizations would be trustworthy and reliable. We all know, however, that we don't live in an ideal world. But if we're dealing with only one familiar corporation operating within the vacuum of one familiar culture, we are at least on common ground in terms of how to handle trust issues.

We have a semi-shared ethic in American business regarding what our employees and employers are supposed to be and do. We generally have a semi-shared sense, too, of when either is failing to meet those expectations, and we have methods and procedures in place to handle those cases. Outside of the vacuum, though, when we embark on partnerships between individuals and corporations, and across cultures, trust issues become even more complex.

The way I see it, trust in business—and maybe in general—can be defined as generally having a realistic sense that a person or an organization is going to behave as we anticipate.

So, if I'm doing business with you and say I trust you, what I'm really saying is that I'm not too concerned that you're going to suddenly do an about-face and act in a way that I never would have expected. You're going to behave in the same way today that you did yesterday, and it's the same way you're going to behave tomorrow.

There's a lot to be said for trust, especially in business, where the stakes are high if people don't behave as we expect them to. Nowhere is this more true that in a cross-cultural, cross-language business situation—and nowhere is behavior less predictable, unless you have studied it with significant depth.

Because you're in a culture (or make that plural!) that is initially unfamiliar, you may often feel that you don't know what to expect next. I never anticipated losing two months of time because I crossed my legs in a meeting. Similar things will probably happen to you. At times it's like walking on eggshells, wondering if you're about to break some rule you've never heard of, or leave the wrong impression by some little gesture. The good news is that there are several ways to create trust in such a situation.

You're probably going to recognize many or all of the suggestions I make. You've encountered them before, most likely. You may not have use for them, as a general rule, since you've been operating in the familiar context of your own company and culture, where trust has, presumably, long since been created—and is in good shape still. In Asia-Pacific, however, all bets are off. You are starting new relationships with new rules, and so I want to review the trust-related ideas I've found to be effective when creating a presence in Asia.

1. **Respect/obedience/honor.** Read and remember the things I've said about these three areas. Nothing will go farther toward establishing and maintaining trust than a clear indication from you, backed up by behavior, that you are respectful of your hosts and honor your partners.

2. **Follow the leader.** The idea is to recognize that your host is the expert in all things Asian, and so you would be wise to follow your host's lead in terms of pace and other behaviors (it's the old "When in Rome" adage).

3. **Don't stretch the truth.** If the statistics aren't great in some area, or if you don't know the answer to a question, tell the truth. Whether you're in Asia or not, stretching the truth (or worse) is ultimately devastating to trust, and you may not get a second chance.

4. **Pipe down.** Americans have a reputation for being loudmouths, although it's generally one or two people giving the rest of us a bad rap. Nonetheless, be aware of your presence in Asia, where loud, pushy, and overbearing rarely go over well (and if they don't go over well, trust doesn't form easily).

5. **Learn the rules.** Put considerable effort into learning both the language and the rules of your host country. While you'll make mistakes, it appears more respectful that you're trying than it does if you don't seem to care enough about impressions to even bother.

6. **Stand on ceremony.** As a rule, the Asian countries emphasize ceremony. Make formal toasts, bring gifts, and otherwise recognize and acknowledge—-very graciously, and very repeatedly—-the generosity and help of your hosts.

The Concept of Face

The idea of losing face or saving face is familiar to most people. In the United States, it's most often related to ego; we're trying to save face when we make a quip about our clumsiness after tripping over our own feet and spilling a drink on someone, for instance (never done that? You're a rare exception!).

In Asia, however, the concept of face is more complicated, and it plays out daily, perhaps even minute-by-minute, in the workplace. The three general considerations related to face are:

- Creating and maintaining face
- Saving and rescuing face
- Losing and damaging face

In the second two categories, there is a division between what we do or what happens to us (i.e., losing face) and what we do to others (i.e., damaging face). We are responsible for not only the creation and maintenance of our own face but for being sure not to damage another's. And we must try to assist the other in saving face if we observe that damage has been done.

What is face? It's the public image we have of ourselves. I emphasize "public," because face isn't about the secret things we know or believe to be true about ourselves. Typically, losing face involves those secret things moving into the public category.

For instance, if you trip and fall walking into a room, you will likely feel that you've lost face. Your public image, that you're graceful and careful, just crashed into your private image, that you're a klutz! You can then try to save face by making a joke, or someone else may try to rescue you (and your face) by distracting others while you get yourself together again.

The subject of face can be fascinating…but what's it got to do with starting up a business in Asia-Pacific? *Everything!*

In perhaps no other culture is the issue of face more present and more in focus than in the Asian cultures. Inextricably related to the issue of personal honor, one's "face" is critical in Asia. In the past, a loss of face was considered a sufficient justification for suicide, if that helps to illustrate just how important the concept is in the Asian countries. To be shamed or embarrassed or humiliated—to lose face—is truly a fate worse than death in the traditional Asian cultures.

What does this mean to you as the person heading into Asia on your great business adventure? How is it going to be evident in your dealings with Asians, and how will it effect the way you do business?

Creating and Maintaining Face

From your first dealing with the Asian market, you are involved in the process of both creating and maintaining face. Creating face simply means developing an image, the way that you wish to be seen in your interactions with others, in this case, with potential Asian partners and customers. We do this every day in business, through our own behaviors and through the press. Companies have many different faces: There are those known as risk-takers, those known to be more conservative, and the like. You have this image in the United States, and, to a greater or lesser extent, your reputation may have preceded you, but there will still be a process in your new corporate world by which you develop or shore up your image, or face.

Just as you are creating face, you are also always actively involved in the process of maintaining face. The only way to do this effectively, I have discovered, is by making your actions consistent with your words. If you say you are a conservative company but then make all sorts of risky moves, you're going to be judged not by what you say but by what you do—and furthermore, you're going to be evaluated based on the inconsistency of your words and deeds.

This is why it is so important for a company to have a clear mission statement and clear goals. If you know "who" you are, corporately speaking, it will be much easier to create and maintain a consistent corporate face.

An important factor in the creation and maintenance of face has to do with the individual people who comprise your start-up team(s). While everyone is going to have a different personality and different approach to doing business, it's key that you have no renegade team members, or people in the start-up effort for reasons inconsistent with the corporate philosophy.

Let me share with you a cautionary tale related to this issue.

When I was first in Asia for Motorola (in Beijing), we were negotiating a contract worth $500 million. Negotiations were halted; the customer team said they needed more technical documentation. We gave them manuals, CDs, everything we had in order to offer further information on the project. After three days of meeting to review the new documents we had given them, the customer team came back and said they couldn't proceed with the project—there wasn't enough information. We'd given them everything we had, and explained that, and the meeting ended on an uncertain note; it appeared that the deal was dead. I started thinking about what was happening. I just couldn't believe that the technical documentation was really behind the stalling. We'd been quite thorough and we knew that the Beijing customer team had enough information to make the necessary decisions. Rather than confronting the customer team directly, I sent one of my team members off to talk privately to members of the customer team. He came back and informed me that the customer team didn't yet have approval from their superiors to sign onto the project. They were, indeed, stalling us. It was made abundantly clear to me, though it was unspoken, that we were being given behind-the-scenes information.

The customer team had created the impression that they were in a position of authority to make this decision on the contract when in fact they were not. They had created a certain "face," or image with us, that face being one of high authority—-when, in fact, they did not possess that authority—-and were actively engaged in maintaining that image.

Losing and Damaging Face

Had I chosen to do what might have been my typical reaction—walking back in and pleasantly but directly confronting the "real" issue, the result would have been a loss of face. The entire structure that had been created, the image, would no longer work for the customer team, since calling them on it would result in the necessity of letting go of the image.

Saying "Hey, listen, guys, I've become aware that you can't actually make this decision, so let's just wait until your superiors check in on it" would have been disastrous, and you can see why. The damage to image would have been permanent—as, I suspect, would the damage to our partnership.

Saving and Rescuing Face

Instead, I went back into the meeting, and pretended I didn't have the information about the dynamics that I did in fact have. I had to pretend that the real issue was the lack of technical manuals, a near absurdity. The customer team had created a face as the decision-makers, the movers and shakers, so I promised to go and look for more tech information, and when they were ready for more, we would return to Beijing with it. By treating what was being said on the surface as the real issue while allowing time for the real issue to get worked out, I was "rescuing face," or giving them the out so that they could save face.

You may find yourself amazed at how often you'll be in a position to do this, and if you choose to brush it aside as silliness, or if you choose to ignore the importance of the issue of face in Asian cultures, you're going to find yourself, again and again, at ground zero.

Within a week we had our approvals, and while I'll never be sure if the customer team knew that I knew they were powerless to move on the deal without superior approval, I am sure that pushing the issue publicly with them would have caused embarrassment, and likely would have been a deal-buster.

The outgrowth of this example, and of the concept of the creation and maintenance of face, is that in your communication you must continually seek out what is not "said" as often, this is what is most important.

In Summary

Let's say you've safely spent your first few weeks in Asia. We've talked about key early issues that I want to summarize quickly before moving on, because we're going to refer to them now and then in the pages to come:

First, take a lot of deep breaths and remain willing to learn new cultures, customs, and ways of doing business.

- Second, be sure to prepare ahead of time. Preparation means:
- learning at least the basics of the language(s) you'll need
- not allowing your expectations to rule you (positive or negative)
- being ready for a full range of emotional reactions to the adventure
- being flexible—with yourself, with others, and with unfamiliar processes

Third, recognize the Relationship Rule and its truisms:

- Bonding and relationship formation is not a race against time
- Lack of commitment doesn't equal disinterest
- Asia is founded on respect for authority

Before we move on to the next chapter of this book, which examines how to create and maintain clear communication both within your business and between you and your Asian partners, I want to remind you of my overriding philosophy, because it's going to come up again and again in the pages ahead.

Doing start-up, no matter how complex, no matter how multifaceted, is never going to be more than you can handle, assuming you remember one simple thing: It's not just a job. *It's an adventure!*

2

Clear Communication Counts

The Day-to-Day Communication Challenges of Start-Up

Just as it is essential to be aware of and sensitive to cultural differences from without and within when heading a start-up effort in a foreign country (or fifty!), it is equally essential to recognize that communication is going to be different from what you may be accustomed to. While language barriers will exist, this is only a small part of what I'm referring to; the real issue is related more to the inherent difficulties involved in creating and maintaining communication networks. With that in mind, I'm going to lay out a plan for setting up your communications in the start-up process, and I'm going to give you specifics about how to handle various barriers and obstacles.

I'm going to break my examination down into three major areas to simplify things and to point out the differences between communication settings. First I'll talk about cross-cultural interpersonal communication, since that's a natural next step from what we've just discussed in terms of culture. Second, I want to examine cross-cultural public communication, the ways in which you create a corporate presence and communication network in Asia. Finally, we'll look at how to set up your internal corporate communications, those processes you'll need to establish both within your start-up team and between the team and the corporate offices that support and maintain the start-up effort.

With the exception of the internal corporate process, the structures you'll set up will be based upon information found in the previous chapter. While I'll refer to that chapter frequently, it's up to you to also figure out ways in which you'll apply issues like "face" to the communication structures and strategies I recommend.

Communication is a perceptual activity, a highly individual process. That is, we communicate based on who we are and how we see the world. As such, it's important that you tailor some of these recommendations to you, specifically. For instance, you may come across a suggestion I make and think that it's not how you would handle a situation. Maybe not. The key is to take the theory or information underlying the suggestion and apply it to the specific situation.

Cross-Cultural Interpersonal Communication

Don't be worried away by the heading above. I'm not going to insist you spend a lot of time talking about your feelings or anything foreign like that! After all, this may be an adventure, but it's still a business book, right?

When I say cross-cultural interpersonal communication, I'm talking about what happens when you sit down and start talking to someone—let's say the Assistant to the Minister of Finance—about those widgets you want to become known for in Asia. Because you're not giving a speech or putting up widget ads on billboards or talking to a committee (yet!), it's *interpersonal* communication. And, because you're an American and the Assistant to the Minister of Finance is Japanese, it's cross-cultural.

You may be thinking, since we've already spent an entire chapter on culture, that the rest is easy. You've given thought to respect and honor and all of those other cultural issues, and when you sit down to have these interpersonal communications, all you have to do is keep those things in mind and you'll be fine.

Not so fast, Kemosabi.

When's the last time you had a really successful interpersonal communication interaction? Think about it. This morning? Six years ago? Either answer is fine, it so happens, because whichever one is true, I'm going to rewrite the script (or explain how I recommend interpersonal communication be handled). I'm also going to ask you to consider what I've learned—added, of course, to what you already know—about communicating across cultures. But let me first up the ante.

Not long after I arrived in Asia, I was in a Muslim country, and we were conducting staff interviews. The way we set things up was that I'd do my interviews in my office, another team member would do his interviews in his office, and several other staff members would work at tables in a rented office back at the hotel. My first candidate, a woman, came in. Because of the noise from surrounding offices—and because it's what I always did during interviews—I closed the door. I wanted to speak with the candidate without distractions or interruptions. I should note that my office had no windows, not even one of those small "door windows" you often see in offices. My candidate was a little nervous, but job candidates usually are a little nervous; so I didn't think anything of it.

After we finished the interview and I ushered her out, the Human Resources Manager came into my office looking worried. We were on a tight schedule, so I didn't really think about what he told me, which was to leave the door open during the rest of the interviews. I did what he said and just kept interviewing candidates. Later in the day when the interviews were finished, I got the complete story: It was not customary in Muslim countries to have a man and woman alone in the same room—not unless someone could see them through a window or an open door. Closing the door, it turned out, was a sign of disrespect, as if I was saying to the candidate that her honor, as well as the customs of her culture, were of no importance to me. In effect, closing the door could be taken as a way of saying I didn't care what anyone thought of this woman (and in the Muslim culture, by the way, the woman would be the one to bear the brunt of my mistake).

I felt very uninformed, as you can imagine, and embarrassed for both myself and the candidate. One heads up was all it took; the discomfort from that mistake was so significant I haven't made it again.

~~~~~~

Cultural Differences and Gender

Gender is still a complex issue, even in the relatively enlightened United States. Like many of the issues I discuss in this book—customs and communication come to mind— gender is made more complex by virtue of the issues taking place outside of home turf. The rules vary from country to country and then within cultures inside of each country, and subtle traditions and cultural mores are harder for the non-native to be attuned to or even aware of.

What I've found is that the role of women in Asia-Pacific varies wildly from country to country. In Japan and Korea, for instance, my impression is that women have to work harder than their male counterparts to be accepted in the workplace; in China and Hong Kong, women are not only accepted in the workplace, but a sure sign of that acceptance is present—-women are expected to perform every bit as well as male colleagues. In Pakistan and India, there have been female leaders even at the highest levels of government: Prime Minister Benazir Bhutto comes to mind. There have also been female icons such as Mother Theresa, of course, but an icon doesn't always translate to be equivalent to a role model or a business leader. In many ways, the presence of icons seems to me to indicate that pedestals are still very much a part of these cultures. It seems to me that when women are put on pedestals, it's difficult for anyone to treat them equally; there's too much protection and care taken, as if women are too fragile to take on these roles for themselves. This would result in a natural exclusion from many positions in business, I would think.

Multiply these differences over fifty different countries, and then throw in different cultures within a country as a rough estimate, and you'll see what women and men trying to work together are dealing with. In a sense, though, the complexity is really not so different from what we deal with in the U.S. workplace, where two genders and multiple cultures interact. This should reassure you; while things can some-times get dicey at home, trying to make sure that equality is a reality at every level of an organization—it's something with which you are familiar.

Given all of these variables when it comes to gender, I would suggest that you create a corporate culture that supports female leadership and that neither explicitly encourages nor implicitly allows different treatment of men and women. The same corporate approach should go for nationalities as well. Operating across Asia-Pacific should result in your having what is likely to be the most culturally diverse team in all of your corporation. Take advantage of the knowledge that this diversity affords and provide the leadership to integrate diversity into your organization. It is not always necessary to follow the "When in Rome" maxim, and this is a good example of a time when you shouldn't. In cultures where women would not be permitted to be in the workplace with men, you will not encounter the issue, because a woman will not apply for a job. It is in cultures where subtle biases exist and are allowed to remain entrenched that you are more likely to find the challenges, and I'd make your corporate and personal position on this clear from day one.

If you're in a country or culture where there are not yet female business role models, provide the support and assistance so that your female employees—ex-pats and locals alike—can become these role models for young Asian women.

By observing you treating women as leaders and/or functional experts, depending on their role and the context, others will come to extend the same treatment if they are not already doing so. By responding with decisive disapproval if harassment or an unequal atmosphere appears to be developing, you will make clear the corporate stance, and you will be respected for your lack of tolerance for unequal treatment.

In the end, dealing with gender or cross-cultural integration issues shouldn't really be so different from how it is back at headquarters. You evaluate people on the basis of their skills, not their sex, and you hire or promote people on the basis of their abilities as well.

~~~~~~

Okay, so maybe communication, cross-cultural or not, is not so simple. And you have a lot riding on this: a lot of money, a lot of face or reputation, a lot of years ahead in which your career trajectory is going to be impacted by how this whole start-up goes. You are, after all, in charge, and so success or failure is ultimately going to fall right in your lap.

When it comes to the importance of communication, it doesn't matter what field you're in—business, medicine, law, you name it. I've done some reading about communication, and the experts in that particular field say we spend 80 percent of our waking hours involved in one form of communication or another. We spend close to half of our waking hours just listening, a major investment of time. And if we're spending nearly half of our time listening, either we're wasting way too much time or else there's a lot being said that we need to catch. I'm guessing, from personal experience, it's some of both, but the part we're interested in, of course, is those times when important information is being imparted, either by you or to you. Whether you're sending or receiving the messages, you're in a key position.

Language Barriers

Let me give you an example of a situation that occurred that illustrates just how key our communication is—an how complex. We had a large contract for servers with a major Chinese customer. We had had several meetings with them to ensure that the project would be successful, and while I didn't attend all project meetings, I was at the last one, and things were just wrapping up for the day. I thought things had gone well, but there was still an impasse that needed addressing. The customer wanted us to produce servers at an accelerated rate, and we were moving as fast as we could already. We'd been up front about this, but because we were still getting pressure to produce more servers faster, I felt it necessary to restate that it just couldn't happen. Meanwhile, it was 5:30 P.M. and everyone wanted to go home. I went ahead and reinforced the fact that their business was important to us, that we'd speeded up the process to the maximum extent possible, and that we'd continue to do everything we could to meet their needs—but we just didn't have the extra servers manufactured yet.

"I'm really sorry," I said apologetically. "Servers take time to build and we have some components that we need in order to complete the build, and we just can't get them today." I shook my head to myself; they knew this, I kept thinking. We were on schedule with our delivery per our agreement with them.

I tried another approach. "Listen, we're working on it, but I know there are still servers to be installed that we have already delivered. You've got enough servers for the optimization team who will be dealing with them; they don't need anything more than that right now. You've as much as said so." We'd discussed this very fact at our last project meeting. They couldn't keep up with installations on the servers they already had; why were they pushing us for more servers so fast?

The meeting had a distinctly uncomfortable air. Tom, the Chinese team's leader with whom we had had the most dealings, looked frustrated and disgruntled. I happened to glance down at Tom's notes during the dead silence that followed my last comment. There it was in black and white:

"Phil says we don't need better service; the service we're getting is good enough for us."

I almost fell off my chair.

"No, no!" I nearly yelled, forgetting myself. "Servers, not service!"

The entire team had understood me to be saying that the customer didn't need or even deserve service any better than what they were already getting. Because they had initially heard my word "server" as "service," they weren't listening for the context in some ways, and I wasn't making any attempt to be careful about how I phrased things; after all, who could get upset over a server? There's nothing personal in that! Selective perception means that we often hear what we're expecting to hear, though, and once they had heard my initial remarks as insulting, everything I said supported that.

Later I realized how fortunate I was in so many ways, not the least of which was that Tom, for some reason, was writing his notes in English; I'd never have seen the mistake had it not been in English.

I was also fortunate that we had built up a relationship over time; I think everyone in that room felt the same amount of relief when the mistake was finally uncovered—in fact, to the credit of the Chinese customers, they still laugh about the incident (I still break out in cold sweats about how close we came to disaster, but that's not an unreasonable response given the circumstances!).

What I took from this meeting—and from countless others, some of which involved even worse translation errors or mistakes resulting from language barriers, was that translation is as much an art as it is a science; good translation involves not just words but body language. You can also gauge the extent to which communication is going awry by watching facial expressions and posture, and by listening to the tone of voice of those involved. As a speaker, you need to speak clearly, because the interpreter needs to understand you clearly, but this still leaves plenty of room for confusion and mistakes. Even if you can't pinpoint where a miscommunication occurred, you can generally recognize that it occurred, and that's the most important thing. By asking participants in a meeting, say, if everyone agrees (once you've summarized), you stand a better chance of avoiding translation errors or similar barriers to effective communication.

I've taken apart the server/service miscommunication many times since then, trying to figure out if there was some point at which I could have caught the problem before feelings were hurt and apologies were needed and everything went awry. There were a few places in the conversation where I should have caught signs of trouble, and I'll talk later about how and where and what to do if you detect such signs. But at the same time, I want to emphasize that my conversation always comes back to two words: servers and service. That incident wasn't isolated, either; I've seen that misunderstanding, with those same two words even, happen time and again. You'll find something similar, probably; depending on your business, certain words will create problems and you'll learn to look out for them after a few incidents, but I have some suggestions that may help you avoid those incidents altogether.

Enunciate

Remember the speech class you had to take in college? You may also remember your professor saying "Ee-Nunn-See-Ate!" when you mumbled your speech in an 8 A.M. class after the previous night's partying. Keep in mind that "standard English" is what people learn in other countries when they learn English. They don't learn "y'all" for "you all" and "Jeet Jet?" for "Did you eat yet?" (These are just a few of the misunderstandings I've heard in cross-cultural situations.)

Avoid Colloquialisms

Even though Americans share one language, we are regional beings, with many slang phrases and phrases that, taken literally, sound pretty odd. Every language has them; the problem arises in cross-cultural communication, when someone who speaks English as a second language, typically interpreting words quite literally, tries to understand them.

A few examples I've seen cause problems, so you'll see what I mean:

What You Say	What You Mean	What Is Heard
You kill me, man!	You are very funny!	You cause my death!
Get outta here!	You've got to be kidding!	Leave this area now!
I could've died!	I was embarrassed!	I was almost killed!
A black sheep...	A nonconformist	A sheep that is black

All of these and plenty more (a "sight for sore eyes" and "burning the candle at both ends" and "looking like you saw a ghost" or "skeletons in the closet") actually managed to make their way into conversations I've heard. Imagine having someone in France call you *mon petit chou.* Unless you're a native, you're going to wonder why you're being called a "little cabbage," and even once you find out that's what it means, you may think it's an insult (it's not; it's an endearment, like calling some "honey").

The same is true in Asia. In Japan, someone might call an expat a "Gaijin," which means a foreigner who is looked down upon, someone who just doesn't get it—-it being a local custom or something of that nature. Know the colloquialism and you'll understand that perhaps you need to examine your behavior. Be sensitive to the fact that languages are hard enough to bridge without adding all of the complex creations we form from words that never make it into English 101. You'll do your host a favor—and that means you'll do yourself and your start-up efforts a favor, too.

Speak More Slowly

This is a fine-line issue. Ever hear someone speaking to a foreign-born person as if the person is stupid? The speaker takes the same tone you heard from your kindergarten teacher, and maybe leans toward the person and smiles encouragingly while talking way too slow and way too loud. The person you're talking to speaks a different language; she or he is neither hearing impaired nor slow on the uptake. Talking too loud and too slowly is insulting.

However, having said that, there's also no reason to dive into conversation at a frenetic East Coast pace. It's an interaction, not the Indy 500. Enunciating will naturally help you to slow your pace, but you can also be aware of the fact that there's no rush and that, ultimately, repeating something three times takes even longer than saying it at a leisurely pace the first time.

Watch for Comprehension

One way to gauge your communication effectiveness is to watch the person with whom you are communicating. Does she or he look confused? If she is taking notes, has she stopped doing so? (This is often a sign that the communication has gotten too confusing or is moving too quickly.) Watch his or her expression for signs of comprehension or confusion.

Summarize

As in any communication interaction, but particularly those that cross cultures, what with all of the opportunities that can be created for confusion, summarize what you've said frequently. At the end of a point, repeat the point and two or three key sentences you've covered within that point. At the end of the whole dialogue, repeat the three or four main points, and try to get the person with whom you're communicating to do the same.

Request Feedback

Ask your listener questions to gauge how effectively the message is getting through. Ask if she or he understands. Ask for him or her to clarify issues that don't make sense.

The server/service example is an interpersonal communication mishap within a small group; the bad news is that it's one of the most prevalent kinds of problems when you're communicating in a foreign culture, but the good news is that it's one of the easiest kinds of problems to avoid. A second typical communication mishap occurs when values or thoughts or feelings get in the way, as they often can in cross-cultural communication.

A Note About Using Professional Translators…

A note I want to add regarding language barriers and translation has to do with translators. For important meetings—those with government officials, for instance—and press conferences, my preference is to have a professional translator available. I also prefer to use someone I've worked with before because (a) the interpreter is at least somewhat familiar with my speech patterns, cadences, accent, and speed; and (b) the interpreter will have had at least some opportunity to become accustomed to the industry lingo and with information about my organization. It's quite common to use someone with good language skills from within an organization ("Why don't we get Joe to translate? Doesn't Joe speak Japanese?") I can't tell you the number of times I've heard statements like that). Why not use Joe and save a little money? Here's why.

First, although this may come as a surprise, **your team member may find this insulting.** She or he may view translation as a support type of function that is beneath his or her level of expertise.

Second, and don't reject this possibility out of hand, **your team member may have an agenda—and it may not be the same as yours.** I raise this issue because I had this experience, and learned my lesson. An employee—our sales manager—was translating for us at a customer meeting. The customer had a complaint about his particular sales representative. The sales manager skimmed right by this little detail, all the while giving the customer—and me—the impression that he was translating the entire exchange.

The agenda behind this was that the sales manager didn't want me to hear the complaint because he was concerned it would reflect poorly on his management of staff (as if his failure to translate truthfully would somehow not reflect poorly on him!). How I found out about it doesn't matter…but it wasn't pretty when I did.

If a customer goes to the trouble to tell me something directly—albeit through a translator—I think that says it's something I should know about.

Third, and the opposite of the prior situation, **your employee may well share more information than you would like.** Every now and then you'll get an employee who believes that they know what you "really" mean…and they do you the supreme "kindness" of sharing that knowledge during the translation. It doesn't matter if it's correct or not, of course.

Fourth, during the translation, **the employee may become aware of information that she or he should not really possess**—because of confidentiality or other reasons.

Over time, I've developed clear reasons, backed up by actual occurrences, for why it's generally unwise to use an employee as a translator.

You too will discover what works best for you over time. I developed a small, reliable network of external translators with whom I like to work. I wish by example alone I could tell you what it's like if you don't have a reliable, good translator—thereby saving you from the experience—but it's an unfortunate fact that you're bound to have a similar experience yourself. I'll just hope that it isn't one, like mine, that you will never forget.

Be Conscious of Communication Filters

It's natural, if you think about it, to apply meanings of your own to every communication interaction. Whenever a person speaks, you're going to hear what he or she says in two ways:

Denotative meanings are the accepted definition of a word or words (i.e., Hong Kong = a city in China comprised of x-million citizens).

Connotative meanings are more complex; they are the ways we have come to interpret words based on our experiences (i.e., Hong Kong = a beautiful city in China where you don't feel worried about your chances at making a start-up work).

My typical approach to a request is a phrase something like this: "I think it would be a great idea if we had a meeting and reviewed the financials, etc." My team knows this that this is really a direction and should be carried out.

I remember a situation that occurred when I was in Beijing that was a direct result of filters, of the ways in which we say something rather than just the content of what we say. We had been in our new building for only a month and were having a ribbon-cutting ceremony in a few weeks. I hadn't been to the building since we'd first taken up residence. I stopped in and was appalled: trash and cigarette butts everywhere, coffee stains all over the carpet—total disarray. From the standpoint of appearances, things just weren't what you'd expect—or want—in a month-old building.

I pointed out some of the problems in my usual manner, mentioned the ribbon-cutting to be held in a few weeks, and ended with, "It would be nice if this place looked better," or something along those lines. Ten days later, I stopped back by the office and it was even worse: more trash, more coffee stains, more cigarette butts. This time I said, "I'm leaving now. I'll be back in the morning. Do whatever it takes to get this place clean." And when I returned in the morning, it was clean.

Because I wasn't initially direct, the local manager at that office heard my initial comments as both an indirect criticism of him and as a vague wish on my part—-neither of which are going to necessarily translate to a direct response. Once the direction was clear, he acted on it. You may see this as a case of resistance of some sort from him, but I know better. I'd never seen him resist instruction before. He was a hard worker who got things done. That's what made me reevaluate the situation, to try to figure out what I was doing that wasn't working. If you always approach situations from the angle that something is going on with the employee, you're going to chase your own tail at times. Nothing with this situation couldn't be fixed by a small shift in language, based on my findings that we were, in fact and in spirit, speaking two languages.

Once I realized that differing "filters" were interfering, my Chinese manager and I sat down for an open discussion in which I explained— clearly and with examples—that it wasn't good enough for us to simply be ready for the ribbon-cutting (his take on matters). Instead, as a world-class company, our facilities should be in world-class shape. Further, it wasn't good enough to be world-class just for the ribbon-cutting. If you're world-class, you're world-class all of the time.

You see the potential problem: If all we used were dictionary definitions, the chances of a foul-up would be minimized, but because we invest words with all sorts of meanings, we end up with the potential for misunderstandings.

In short, you can do three things to help avoid this problem. First, **try to stick to the denotative, or dictionary, level when you're speaking**

across cultures. This is easier said than done, because we all invest words with various meanings without even realizing we're doing so. However, avoiding communication behaviors such as sarcasm or dead-pan humor, both of which rob a word of its dictionary meaning, can help. Both sarcasm and dry humor depend on complex familiarity with a language, since their outcome relies on the conflict between what is said and what is not said. This conflict is something we have in a native language but rarely in a second, acquired language.

Next, **examine your "filters" carefully.** By that I mean it's important to examine your perceptions as they relate to other cultures. We all have beliefs about other cultures—this is not necessarily a bad thing; this does not mean that you have prejudices, or that you will behave in ways detrimental to people of cultures different from you're own. If you believe, for instance, that Hong Kong is a hurried, pressured place, this is not necessarily a negative. What can be a negative is that your communication can unconsciously reflect (and create or reinforce) that belief. You can communicate your way right into self-fulfilling prophecies. By becoming aware of your beliefs, you can more easily set them aside and slow down; it is entirely possible that your hurried, pressured communication explains your perception of Hong Kong.

Finally, it is also entirely possible, as it was in my case, that your communication is not direct enough to get through. This may be related to the language differences, of course, but it can also be related, I believe, to the fact that some of the general team or management team you're hiring may not have worked with a foreigner before. As a result, your team members are also learning the subtle differences of which we've been speaking. (Add to this the fact that you may have newly appointed managers who are still learning corporate-speak and corporate processes, and you've got team members taking hairpin turns on a major learning curve.) Therefore, my third piece of advice about how to deal with filters is to **be direct: eliminate the nonessential fillers when it's important to impart information or instructions.** When you're bridging the span between two languages, you may find that you have to cut out some of the extraneous words, the niceties like "I think it would be better if" and "I'm wondering if" and "What if we..." and so on. While they grease the social wheels, they also can clutter a sentence and require a focus on words that aren't key to the concept. When the goal is to impart information or instructions, pare it down.

Wishful Thinking

Another obstacle I've seen get in the way of communication time and again during start-up efforts is a process that looks to me like wishful thinking. Living and working in a culture that is foreign to us can be difficult. I've watched others make this mistake, and I've made it myself: communicating as if there are no differences from what we're accustomed to. Maybe it's a distortion on political correctness, because if we behave differently, doesn't that imply that we believe there are differences? And if there are differences, does that mean one is better than the other? The answer is simple: no.

When languages and cultures differ, it's not politically incorrect to recognize that. Failure to do so is nothing but hiding your head in the sand, with the obvious negative results.

If by some strange chance you want to see a start-up effort fail, just go back and read the first chapter of this book and look at the cautions I've offered in terms of cultural differences—and then ignore them. Pretend there are no differences, that hierarchy and honor and respect don't matter. Soon, maybe they won't matter, since you may find yourself on a plane headed back to the United States. Fortunately, wishful thinking is fairly easy to eliminate; it just involves a steady commitment to reality, something you've already got plenty of practice at since you've made it this far in the business world.

Wishful thinking often plays out in a casual approach to business relationships. If you imagine that in the Asia-Pacific you can sit around and shoot the breeze with superiors and subordinates alike, perhaps throwing in amusing barbs, you're likely to encounter trouble. It's not atypical for expatriates, in their lonelier moments, to do precisely this sort of thing, trying to recreate familiarity in a social sense. It's wishful thinking because it expresses a desire to be back in the States, where you know what's what, where things aren't so complicated—but that's not reality. You've got to let go of the need for things familiar. Focus your energies on adapting rather than resisting. You're dealing with something much larger than you or your start-up team or your corporate clout; you're dealing with the way a culture has done things for many, many years.

When you're feeling most cut loose, most disconnected from what you know, the worst thing you can do is to retreat to the safety of how you've always done things. Behaving outside of the practices of the society in which you're moving will further isolate you from that society. Whether it's communication or some other practice we're talking about, keep in mind the essence of what I'm saying here: Resistance is not only futile; it's potentially disastrous.

Undercutting Authority

Another problem occurs when start-ups don't recognize or adapt to the formalized structures within which they're now communicating.

Over time, you will develop networks and connections within Asia. You will come to know certain people upon whom you can rely, people you can go to behind the scenes to get information on dynamics or processes or other essential areas. Early on, though, you're not going to have these connections, and it can make the start-up more complicated. You probably have an established network at home, so you're probably going to feel at loose ends until you develop that in your new home. This is normal, and it will change naturally and gradually.

In the meantime, though, I've seen people make the mistake of trying to rush those kinds of connections, and it doesn't work. Behind-the-scenes networking occurs only once trust has been established, and you can't rush trust. You have to simply operate as best as you can while your actions make a case for why you should be trusted.

I've seen people who believed that their personal magnetism could overcome Asia's often formal communication structures. Maybe they approached a foreign team member for the "back story" on a situation, only to be rebuffed, since what was requested was that the foreign team member tell tales to an "unknown quantity." Not only is a loss of face involved when this occurs, but I also think it damages trust, because it's clear that someone is trying to short-circuit the formalized networks and hierarchies. I'd compare this type of situation to asking a stranger for a favor. They're going to back away just a bit, because there's no established relationship yet. While your intentions in bypassing a cumbersome formalized network were probably good, the appearance of impropriety is often as powerful as the impropriety itself.

I'll give you an example so you see what can happen.

In the hectic start-up phase, it's difficult to get to really know your staff's staff. You're frantically busy much of the time, and in addition, you're generally interacting with your own staff. It's not that people aren't friendly toward each other—if anything, they may be more so, strangers in a strange land easing the transition. Trust, though, is still forming; it's only natural that the deeper levels of your work relationships aren't established; knowing this, you don't even worry about it, knowing it will form over time.

One day early in this stage I was at our center in Malaysia. The head of our engineering staff approached me with a problem: We were facing huge delays in getting a small part we needed to build desktop computers, and his boss, the center's Managing Director, was out of the office. The engineer had been trying to work out this problem for weeks, but now that I was here, he thought maybe I could make some progress. I'm afraid I let my "Leader Ego" interfere, and I assured him that I would take care of it. I placed a call to one of the supplier's team members—not the leader, and I did that on purpose, as recommended by another team member.

I invited the supplier's rep for tea at our center that day. We met and had tea, and my thinking was running along these lines: He's going to be pleased and flattered by the attentions, and when I ask him if he can't speed up the manufacturing of the part, he's going to do it. We had a jovial, extremely friendly meeting, and I slipped the question into our conversation near the end. He seemed taken aback, and dubiously said he'd do what he could.

Maybe you can guess the outcome. He didn't know me, but what he did know was that I bypassed the formalized communication and authority structure. He also knew that I wasn't as interested in getting to know him and building a relationship as I was in trying to get something moving on the project, which, once you give it a moment's thought, is really insulting. Word got back to his superior, not surprisingly, and relationships were chilly for some time—I had, after all, caused his superior to lose face when I bypassed him. Rather than speeding up the manufacturing of the small part, I slowed it down; where it had been taking two to three weeks to get each shipment, suddenly it was taking over a month.

I learned my lesson in that one experience, and I've seen it repeated time and again with others. The specific lesson was that I should have contacted the leader at our supplier and visited with him. During the visit, I should have focused on business matters and shared with him how pleased I was with them as a supplier. I should have eventually brought the conversation around to them as a supplier, talking about our future business relationship and asking for a favor for our customers (in getting help with this part we needed). This approach would have been direct—and that's unbeatable—and it would have been addressed to the correct person at the correct level. My guess is that the response to this type of approach would have been far more positive than the response to the approach I actually used.

Authority structures tend to be quite strong in Asia, and while there are variations within each country, and even regional differences, the bottom-line rule remains the same: Operate within the communication network and authority structure that already exists until you have had time to adapt to the culture.

How much time is enough? When is a good point for you to introduce informal, behind-the-scenes networking, for instance? My practice these days is to wait until the structure is breached by someone within it. When someone comes to me with information, or when someone indicates a willingness to help me informally, that's when I know enough time has passed to begin to create informal networks. Until then, I stick with the program, and you'll be better off if you do the same. Remember, however, that you need to be very open so you can be approached. While you will stay within a more formal structure for starters, you want the people with whom you communicate to feel comfortable making the shift into less formalized communication. The way to do so is to encourage others to approach me, and to respond favorably when they do—it's as simple as that.

Over-familiarity

While this next potential problem can occur both interpersonally and in the more structured arena of public communication, it is most likely to take place in an interpersonal setting, either between two people or within a small group. It's a natural outgrowth of what we just discussed, wherein you approach someone outside of the strictures of the formal hierarchy. Most often, what is behind this is a sense that it's okay to be familiar with someone, to have a relationship with them that isn't bound by the rules and formality of the hierarchy. This is frequently, to put it mildly, a big mistake.

Because the Asian countries are typically relationship oriented, as I discussed in Chapter One, there are all sorts of rules, spoken or, more often, unspoken, about how relationships are "done" in Asia. Adult relationships can have a graceful formality to them, even those that have existed since childhood. This formality may seem, from the outside, to inhibit closeness or honesty, but as I have spent more time in Asia and have come to understand more about the relationships, I have come to have a deep sense of admiration and respect for how relationships are built and maintained.

The respectfulness upon which Asians build their relationships is something I find fascinating and positive. What it means for the American businessperson, though, is learning a whole new approach, quite different from the State's often more casual, informal, and familiar approach.

The typical Asian relationship—friendship, familial, or business connection—maintains an interpersonal distance. The person who overdiscloses, for instance, is likely to be considered odd and emotionally sloppy, for want of a better term. To share private information with an Asian counterpart about the state of one's marriage, say, is considered to be extremely poor form and in extremely poor taste. It just isn't done. To flirt with an Asian of the opposite sex in a business setting, no matter how innocuous the flirtation, also isn't done—and the behavior likely won't end up being innocuous. Flirtation is a clear sign of familiarity, and so you see the conflict. This leads me to my next point, one that varies from country to country in Asia, but that has a similar base throughout the continent.

Gender Complexities

In my experience, and this may surprise you, I've found Asia to be generally more gender-neutral than the United States. What I mean by this is that in a number of the countries in Asia, you'll find men and women in the workplace without the same degree of complication that can sometimes occur in the United States because of antiquated belief systems and hierarchies.

Certainly some Asian countries have not included women in the corporate or government workforce to as great an extent as we see in the U.S.. In addition, the Muslim countries, of course, have different beliefs and practices, many of which translate into gender issues. I've discussed this in more detail, of course, earlier in this chapter. However, as it relates specifically to communication, and as a generalization for all of Asia (for all other countries, for that matter, at least until you're extremely confident about the rules of communication—verbal and nonverbal), here's the deal: avoid touching, hugging, or greeting a member of the opposite sex with a kiss. For that matter, in countries with more extreme religious values, you would not even initiate a conversation with a woman. To ignore social rules regarding touch, in particular, signals over-familiarity and breaches a basic cultural value.

The ways in which gender becomes a part of the communication process and the ways in which the potential for miscommunication occurs are complex. The conclusion I've reached is pure common sense. While you'll want and need to learn the specifics about culture and customs in any country in which you do business, the most important thing you can do is to be vigilant: Be vigilant in terms of sensitivity to potential differences and be vigilant in terms of awareness of the responses of others so you can correct errors and shortcut near misses. Even in countries in which there are no surface attitudes or moral imperatives regarding women in the workplace, you're going to find, at the very least, some degree of protectiveness toward the women in the culture, and that will result in differences in terms of customs and behaviors.

In other words, then, treating everyone as an equal in the workplace is far and away your best bet. If you do so, and are gender-blind, you will do well. Keep in mind that you're a foreigner and that you represent your company; anything—and everything—you do reflects back onto your company. By watching you, others will decide what kind of company you have.

The United States has many more laws related to gender issues and sexual harassment than do the Asian countries, I found. Utilizing the basic guidelines set out in our corporate practices—those guidelines being founded on common sense and equality for all—worked well for us and continues to do so.

The key is communication. You must be completely clear with your employees about your expectations, both verbally and in writing, and you must respond quickly and in detail when those expectations are not met. This is true in terms of any disciplinary problem, of course, but there's often more at stake with an issue like fraternization. You don't have to agree with a country's stance toward women—that paternal protectiveness, for instance—but if you're doing business in the country with that stance, you'd be making a big mistake not to go along with it, and so would your employees.

Cross-Cultural Public Communication

Even as you're working on setting up networks of interpersonal communication in Asia, you will be developing a public presence. You may not start off with a blitz of publicity, depending on your strategy, but you will begin to make your presence known. In this section, I want to talk about how to do that: what works and what doesn't work and why. If you get a handle on why certain things work and don't work, you'll be in a better position to create your own communication strategies in Asia.

Existing Communication Channels

There is a huge range of quality and access to the media in Asia. In smaller, less-developed countries, you'll find a single television station, always government-run, without advertising. In Japan, China, Australia, and other large countries, you'll find something that looks more familiar to you: a competitive media environment where you can purchase advertising airtime. Radio closely mirrors what you'll find with television. Print media, press conferences, and trade shows are often going to end up being your best bet when it comes to publicity. You'll be able to garner a few articles, probably, about your company's start-up in Asia, and you'll certainly be able to purchase advertising space.

When it comes to public relations and advertising (I talk about the media and public relations more specifically in Chapter Four), I think the wisest thing your company can do in terms of preparing for and creating an awareness of the complexities and realities of a start-up is to make a corporate decision to treat corporate communications, public relations, branding, and advertising as you would any other corporate enterprise; in other words, be sure there is a return on your investment.

You must treat this area as central to your business plan, not as some thrown-together add-on or afterthought.

Media is expensive in Asia, and you must establish return-on-investment goals and measurements for every dollar you spend on public relations. If you don't, you will likely find yourself "spending silly" and not achieving your goals.

Media Options

Because the media differs drastically from country to country within Asia, it would be impossible to provide you with a specific description of what's available where. The region has several good public relations and advertising firms you can call upon. Over the past six or seven years I have seen them develop more expertise, which will make your start-up efforts even easier than it was back when. They can give you ideas and direct you to the best opportunities for public relations in the region.

Additionally, familiarize yourself with the options available to your company: television, radio, print. The core print places to advertise in Asia include the Asia Wall Street Journal, the Economist, and the Far East Economic Review. CNN and STAR TV are good television bets, but these regional-coverage mediums may be too general; country-specific media could actually be better for your business.

There are also more creative means for publicizing your presence in a region: You can become associated with a regional event, for instance, or you can sponsor a seminar. In Chapter Four I discuss the Internet, which is taking off in Asia, as another great source for exposure and advertising.

The bottom line: Find out what is available, adapt your messages to the market, and determine which media alternatives give you the best return.

Benevolent Publicity

A terrific way to get publicity, regardless of the country you're in, is to get your company involved in the community. Sponsor an education center or school, rebuild a youth center, provide medical supplies to a clinic if you're in a less-developed area...regardless of how you get involved, this is the best way to create a presence in Asia. Here's why:

Giving is highly valued in Asia. As a rule, gifts are expected on arrivals and departures, beginnings and endings, accomplishments, you name it. Be sure to read carefully the section about giving in Chapter Four so you get the details, but remember that corporate giving not only creates a benevolent image of your company, it gives back to the region that will be giving so much to you.

Adapting Your Message to the Market

Marketing is going to be a bit different in Asia than in the United States. What comes to my mind immediately is how Dell had me go into Asia-Pacific countries that had very few phones, countries that, in some cases, had electrical challenges, and others in which mail systems simply did not work. Our challenge—if you can imagine—was to create a market for high-end personal computers in these countries.

Well, of course, we didn't even try. Our strategy was to implement our competitive competencies in the countries where our opportunities for success would be the highest. This also happens to be where the majority of the PC business was located, although not necessarily where all three billion plus people lived. Sometimes you have to give the market time to catch up with you; to do otherwise would be foolish. It seems obvious, of course, but many, many businesses have failed in Asia and across the world when they tried to be everything to everyone. In Asia, pick your target markets and start there, then expand as demanded. History is littered with businesses that didn't bridge the gap between the product available and market needs.

Internal Corporate Communications

You undoubtedly have a clear internal corporate communication process in place at headquarters and between headquarters and your various field offices in the United States, or would like to think so. With the advent of electronic communication, what used to be the standard for internal corporate communication now seems as inefficient as writing on stone tablets. The communication structures you have in place are a good starting point—but not the end point—for the processes you will need to support your start-up efforts.

Here's why it's essential that you create a project-specific plan for communication during your start-up. Start-ups, regardless of whether they're taken with a risk-aversive or risk-friendly approach, occur in fits and starts; it's the nature of the beast. You'll have days during which nothing moves, and then you'll go through wild, roller-coaster-ride days and weeks when each moment seems to bring a new shift. Without clear communication, both internally to the start-up team and between start-up and corporate, you won't be able to respond and react to these shifts, and you certainly won't be able to make proactive moves, since you'll always be playing catch-up, trying to track down your team and corporate for decision-making, for instance.

On the other hand, if you have clear decision-making processes in place, and clear methods by which you handle communication about those decisions and changes, you will be in a much better position, both internally and externally. With as seamless as possible a process established, you'll also make a much better impression on potential Asian partners. Here's why:

- *You will appear proactive rather than reactive.*
- *You will be in a position to fine-tune responses along the way rather than having to hold off on all decision-making until corporate can be reached, thus potentially missing important details.*

- *You will be able to instantly respond to potential customers, since immediate answers from corporate, when needed, will not slow down your response time to your customer base.*
- *You will be kept up-to-date on corporate changes that impact your start-up, thus avoiding costly or "face"-damaging mistakes with customers.*
- *You will be in a position to handle problems quickly, before ripple effects result from untended-to issues.*

I say all of this to impress upon you the essential nature of communication, particularly electronic communication. In retrospect, the early days of your start-up are likely to be hectic; communications with your team, their team, your headquarters, and global peers may not get the attention they deserve. I was just too busy, in the case of my own start-up, but "out of sight out of mind" can really put a strain on relationships, especially since you are counting on the strength of these relationships during your start-up.

Several methods of communication we utilized in the early days of our start-up carried us through the formation years: weekly briefing reports on the start-up group's activities, weekly conference calls with the staff, email, individual telephone calls, monthly "town hall" meetings, personal visits, quarterly visits to headquarters, and development of our intranet site. These ideas are probably not new to you. What we found is that the more frequently we used these methods and the more we combined them, the better our communications network within the group and with headquarters. Remember, you are probably on the other side of the world from headquarters; if you don't keep them updated, you will create a risk for yourself and your organization. You've heard the ad which says "Don't leave home without it"— nowhere is it more true than when talking about a communication structure that involves email. I've come to rely on email more heavily than even the telephone.

If you treat internal and external communication as something that gets done when and if everything else gets done (it never does), you're going to find yourself regretting that approach—big time. From cover-you-back issues to idea exchange to public relations to employee stability, clear communication is essential. It counts.

3

Managing Reality

Team Support and Staffing Issues

Perhaps the most important decision you will make once you have committed to bringing your business into Asia-Pacific concerns the start-up team. How you determine who will be on the team will have a profound impact upon the success of your start-up.

Your start-up team will be a microcosm of your company's organizational culture, ethics, and outlook. As a result, anyone on the outside looking in—customers, local citizens, and government officials, for instance—will judge your entire organization by the positive or negative actions of a few people, and in many cases when team members are under tremendous stress. You won't have the luxury of a large corporate culture that can absorb and shelter to the occasional weak link or problem employee or downright bad apple.

In more human terms, the team will consist of very real people with very real personalities, which can become magnified in light of the ongoing stress and intense change a foreign start-up entails. Neither the individual nor the systemic realities can be ignored when you're involved in a start-up effort; to ignore either is to borrow trouble, and you're already going to have your hands full even if everything goes off without a hitch. You certainly don't need to add to your responsibilities with trouble areas created by benign neglect or worse.

Because so much is riding on the start-up team, you are going to want to focus a substantial amount of energy on two related areas: First, you need to figure out how to choose a team; second, you need to be clear about what (and who) will work out in the start-up—and what (and who) won't. I've had lots of experience on both sides of the ocean, and I can tell you that you need a different kind of person for your start-up than you need on home soil. Certainly there will be overlap; whatever continent you're on, for instance, you're going to want staff with superb technical abilities. But huge differences exist between what works in a familiar, domestic setting and what works in the foreign adventure when it comes to personality, work style, and other issues.

CHOOSING YOUR START-UP TEAM

The question of how to choose your start-up team has answers that are purposefully generic; in other words, you can apply these thoughts regardless of the type of business you're running and regardless of where you'll be located. In addition, the size of your start-up team won't be an issue as you continue planning how you will go about choosing team members. You know how many people you'll need—and you'll probably make do with less. The practicalities of how to choose these people won't impact quantity—just as quantity shouldn't impact how to make your decisions, to a significant extent. Methods for choosing team members stress quality issues, and like anything in business, or, for that matter, in any area of effort, quality far outweighs quantity.

You'd think you could just look around at corporate, maybe at a few of the regional offices that have a reputation for being on the move and hard-charging, then pick out your stars in each place, make some offers, and see what happens. You're bound to get at least some of the best people with that approach, and that's what you want in a start-up, the best people. Right?

While it's true, obviously, that you want a team with competence and a solid working knowledge of the organization and the product or service you're offering, it is not necessarily true that you want your corporate stars lighting up the start-up team. In order to come up with the team that will best serve your organization by ensuring the greatest chance of success, you really need to look at the following general personal and personality factors: technical competence, communication and social competence, balance, and an ethical and moral center. You will probably also discover, as I did, that you cannot find all of your start-up team members within the company. I recruited a few team members—all people with start-up experience—from other companies.

Technical Competence

As mentioned earlier, technical competence must be taken into account when selecting members of the start-up team. I viewed my start-up team much as a coach might view the first string of a football team: I had a limited number of slots available, so I was looking, in part, for people who represented a wide range of skill areas. To the extent possible, I was also looking for people who had the technical comfort and competence to be and become skilled generalists as well. Whatever your product or service, you will have certain skill groupings that are essential, and if you find yourself in an area where you cannot recruit the local skill you need, it is essential to bring your own talent. As an Information Technology company, Dell is fortunate to have any number of employees who are not only highly trained and highly skilled in specific and specialized areas of I.T., but also to have employees who are generalists when it comes to technology. But even with all of this talent, I still needed to recruit outside of the company. The benefit to the team has been that we have always had more than just the one expert in a technological area—and we've also had technology-minded employees who could get the office phone system programmed, set up our LAN, and troubleshoot when I.T. problems arose while, say, a certain specialist was away. You will have to determine the essential skill areas, but keep in mind the benefits of having a generalist in your field on board, and don't let the hunt for a technological genius obscure the reality of your search for team members.

Communication and Social Competence

You've read "Asia Doesn't Exist" and "Clear Communication Counts," and I hope that in those two chapters I convinced you that cultural issues and communication complexities will be a part of your everyday life in a foreign start-up. I want to convince you of these things not to worry you but to give you the chance to take social and communication skills into serious consideration as you choose team members.

You cannot truly train someone to become socially adept. You can certainly help someone overcome anxiety about social situations, or move past a paralyzing fear of public speaking, or better cope with amyriad other areas in which communication and social interaction can create obstacles, but the extrovert tends to be consistently so, and the introvert is not likely to appear at the office one day and suddenly become the chief confessor and confessee in the crowd. However, it is not necessary to be a certain type to be socially competent; instead, it is necessary to possess a certain ability to recognize one's impact on others and to be sensitive to cultural issues and signals from others regarding communication.

Here's what you're looking for: team members who are generally well liked, generally accepted by peers, supervisors, and employees, and generally comfortable with and responsive to customers. In other words, generally really nice people. Ask for opinions from people you trust to be discreet, and observe the potential team member in his or her interactions with others. Review personnel files, of course, but look beneath the surface for any commentary on social issues or conflict-management styles and outcomes. Most important, trust your instincts.

Balance

Balance can be a complex issue, but what I'm referring to here is both a personal and a personality quality that leads a person to have a good balance of the professional, personal, and other areas of his or her life. You don't want a team member who routinely overextends himself or herself, because this would likely indicate a lack of ability to create and maintain limits and balance.

Instead, you're looking for someone who recognizes that there is more to life, for instance, than work. Perhaps the potential team member is involved in exercise or a sport. Certainly she or he will give indications of a healthy, ongoing social life with friends, family, and within the community, and will have opinions about things other than issues related to work. She or he will mention recent events and will sometimes be able to view them, even those that are frustrating, with a sense of humor.

Why is balance important enough to include in the top four factors of which you should be aware? Several reasons. First, if you choose a team member who is out of balance—a workaholic, let's say—when something goes wrong at work, everything gets thrown off because work is the central and consuming focus of that person's life. Second, balance will help your team member tremendously during the start-up as stress builds; because of other sources of tension release and satisfaction, she or he will be able to escape and come back refreshed and ready to work again.

Ethical and Moral Center

Finally, a clear sense of ethics and morality is essential for your team members. Let me define what I mean by this, because it's easy to assume I'm suggesting a team member should have some specific set of morals, and I'm not. What I'm saying is, provided your team member has a clear moral compass, something that obviously guides him or her through complex situations, you will be in a much better position to trust that the employee will not put the organization in harm's way. The same holds true for ethics—but even more so.

There are any number of different cultures when it comes to business, and in some cultures, corruption, kickbacks, bribes, and other activities are common. I'm not suggesting these are commonplace in every country or territory within Asia-Pacific, but they are present in some.

Nonetheless, it is essential that your team members have ethics of the highest standards, ethics that can go from region to region, regardless of the local business culture, and remain intact. While in most contexts you want employees who are not black-and-white thinkers, who have the ability to be more sophisticated and subtle in their thinking and judgment, when it comes to ethics, to the extent possible you *will* want team members who do not see shades of gray.

Obviously, these four considerations—technical competence, communication and social competence, balance, and an ethical and moral center—are not the only factors you'll take into account as you begin the process of identifying potential team members. However, they're a good foundation and starting point for both identifying and ruling out people for the team, and if no factors beyond these were taken into consideration, you would still find yourself with a solid team that was likely to get past the typical personal obstacles associated with foreign start-ups and move your organization forward with grace and skill.

The Dream Team

Having considered these general factors, let's look at personality types and qualities you want to look for as you begin the process of selecting team members.

The Adventurer

You probably could have predicted that I'd consider the Adventurer to be a great team member, but let me back it up with reasons just so you don't think I've included it in order to get myself on the team for all time. What the Adventurer has that his or her opposite doesn't have is a high tolerance for change and unpredictability and…well, adventure! The high tolerance level for change and unpredictability will give you an employee who has more patience than someone else might have, and patience is more than a virtue during a start-up; it's a sanity saver and a team-building skill that can create near miracles.

The Old Hand

In recruiting team members, I look for experience in three areas: within the region, within the company, and within the industry. If you are part of a fast-growing company that is new to the region, as Dell was, you may not find any potential team members with all three bases of experience; I didn't. Two out of three was the best I could find, but even if some of your team members have only three or four months of experience with start-up or in the region, that's a head start on someone who has none.

Even if the experience your team member has is in recreational traveling in the region—or, for that matter, in another region—you've still got someone who is familiar with travel and cultural differences and other issues that can occur for ex-pats. I've noticed that ex-military, as well, can make great team members; they often have the structured, organized background that makes for a good fit with a start-up effort, and the ability to both develop and follow through on detailed plans is always a bonus.

The Smart Cookie

The team member who is realistic and practical will understand certain key factors about the start-up. It is time limited, and so any challenges are finite. Success must be measurable, so results count. They are just one piece of the puzzle, and if they don't do their piece, the puzzle is incomplete—and so they do their piece. Their pride comes not from status but from accomplishment—and so they accomplish. They recognize that they cannot make this effort work alone—and so they enlist other team members and make great team players.

The Team Builder

Because the team will be in a foreign region, starting relationships from scratch, I've found that the people who do the best on a team are those who have a strong sense of confidence in themselves (this carries them through the early days, before they have friendships that provide positive feedback) and are friendly (this helps to form those relationships). While I don't think it's essential that someone be outgoing, since introverted types make friends, too, I do think that a person who is very inwardly focused will have a much more difficult time adapting, and what is difficult for the team members tend to create difficulties for the team.

The Disaster Team

What about the qualities that should make you think twice—or even rule out all thought—about bringing someone onto the team? You'll have your own experiences, personality types you know you just can't work with. You'll want to give these some thought to be sure you're not creating too narrow a base for potential team members, but the bottom line is that if you believe a certain characteristic is destructive, it probably is…and even if it isn't, you probably don't need to deal with it while you're trying to handle all of the other elements of the start-up.

Here, then, is a handful of the personality types I think can cause the worst problems for a start-up team and the whole effort if they're allowed to run wild.

The Escapist

Beware the team member who isn't running toward the adventure but is instead running away from something. It may be a personal problem—a marital breakup, financial woes, pressures in the regular job—or just a general escapist approach to life, never committing to anything for too long. Either way, this person is a poor risk for you. The Escapist, because he (or she) is only there for the escape, a short-term deal, is going to be much more focused on what the start-up can do for them than on what they can do for the team and overall effort.

The Expert/Authority

It's one thing to be the Expert/Authority…if you are the Expert/Authority. Some people, however, have an inflated, unrealistic view of their value and contributions. This can result in a distorted view of the degree of authority and autonomy they have. The person who misunderstands and misrepresents his or her power in the workplace (and power can derive from expertise or from vested authority) is also likely to make inappropriate independent decisions and to take actions that have not been cleared by the real authorities.

The Expert/Authority creates a threat to the chain of command because he or she undercuts the actual authority and can create questions with customers and others not in the authority loop regarding who is in charge. Additionally, the Expert/Authority is a potential source of loss of face—embarrassment—for the management team and for the organization as a whole.

The Homebody

Someone who doesn't have an adventuresome streak will be ill prepared to separate from his or her comfort zone, whether that's the family or the familiar grocery store, and that's going to make life a lot more difficult both for the team member and the team. Precious time and energy will be pulled away from the team listening to the discomfort and complaints of the person who isn't comfortable in his or her new surroundings. There's nothing wrong with being a Homebody, but it's not a good match for the start-up team.

The Emotional Wreck

There's always someone who takes great pride in telling everyone around them how difficult life is. Their family is always suffering some sort of upheaval; there's always a chaotic emotional situation in the works with a friend or colleague; a simple medical test that anyone might have is dragged out for weeks so this person can agonize over whether a terminal illness lurks. You know the type; there's one in every workplace. When you see the Emotional Wreck approaching with a job application, don't walk. Run. Run fast. The fact is, you and your team members will have plenty to deal with without the addition of your own personal office soap opera airing 24/7.

The Renegade

This person has a general dispute with authority. He or she may not acknowledge this, and is likely to be extremely resistant to discussing it openly or, heaven forbid, dealing with it directly and in practical terms. Instead, the Renegade's preferred modus operandi is to sometimes make a show of listening and agreeing with instructions (sometimes the Renegade doesn't even make this effort) and then to proceed with his or her own plans, whatever they may be. On occasion, those plans will actually benefit the organization, but this is a fluke, and in any but the most superficial way, no matter what the results, the Renegade has damaged the organization by failing to accept the realities of it. This sends a message to other employees, a message that can't be positive, and can often waste the time of management as they are left to clean up public relations messes, soothe ruffled customer feathers, and, in the worst-case scenario, try to repair any permanent damage.

Regarding the qualities you should be looking for in potential team members, the above is by no means an exhaustive list of the qualities to avoid. I summarize the positive attributes of a person who focuses on how to make the start-up, the company, and their family successful. Use both the positives and the negatives as starting points as you begin to consider certain people for your start-up team and you will find that often, whether during interviews or less formal dealings, potential candidates will rule themselves out with almost no assistance from you. You, then, can help persuade potential team members to sign on by emphasizing the positives and by focusing on the adventure, while still presenting a realistic picture of foreign start-up.

A Hint: Look, Listen, and Learn

What I've learned is that one key set of behaviors on my part is essential for every phase of handling staff issues, from selecting team members to helping prepare those team members for the move away from the familiar and into the adventure to dealing with ongoing obstacles and issues once the team is settled into the new region.

My task—to look, listen, and learn—is too simple to work, but it does. Everything I've told you about selecting team members, and everything I'm about to tell you about preparing the team for the move and dealing with obstacles and problems within the team once the move is made, relies on your ability to keep a finger on the pulse of your team members. If you're not sensitive to what's going on with your team, nothing I say will make any difference, because you won't know how to implement it. You've got to watch for signs of conflict or trouble if you're going to keep the team together.

Look: Keep your eyes on the details and the big picture. Be sure to watch potential team members at work or during the recruitment process for signs that their words might be inconsistent with their behaviors. Later, be sure to observe signs of your employees settling into their new job and home, making connections, getting more comfortable. Listen: Be sure to listen for inconsistencies, employee comfort, and positive changes in perspective over time. Learn: Use the information you've gathered to help your team and your organization continue to grow, and for further recruitment or future start-up opportunities.

Significant Others

You'd love Buddy Griffin if you met him. Everybody loves Buddy Griffin, even the folks who are initially taken aback by the way he approaches complete strangers, sticking out his arm for a hearty handshake as the recipient stands there unsure of who or what Buddy Griffin is. Buddy is one of those wide-open Irishmen, the kind who is exactly as he seems to be: a guy with unbridled enthusiasm, sincerity, and an engaging, compelling personal warmth that he extends to everyone who crosses his path. Even with the most reserved strangers, it only takes Buddy a time or two to win them over, and it's no surprise; Buddy is one of the warmest, most gregarious people you could ever meet. He loves change; he loves a challenge; he's the kind of person who can walk into a completely new, totally unfamiliar situation and make it his in minutes. He's also technically competent, and the combination of these factors is why I'm so fortunate to have had Buddy on my start-up team.

Once I was certain Buddy was up for the adventure, I was so delighted that I took him out to dinner, along with his wife, Maureen, to celebrate. I just assumed that everyone was excited about this newest challenge—the move to a foreign country, the chance to make something from nothing. Assuming this, the last thing I expected was what happened: At dinner with Buddy and Maureen, it became very apparent that Maureen was not happy with me. I'd even say she appeared angry.

"How could you do this?" she said. "How could you change our life like this?" She talked about their children, the extended family that would be left behind, the upheaval, her fears. "If I'm doing something bad to your family," I interrupted, still stunned by Maureen's distress, "we'll stop right now. But," I added, "I need Buddy. What can I do to help?"

We talked for a long time that night, and I was able to assuage some of Maureen's fears. They decided to maintain two households—one in Ireland and the other in Malaysia—and to travel back and forth so their youngest child could complete his education. I also suggested to Maureen that every six months they pick a place in Asia and get away from work and the pressures of the start-up. Buddy found that idea intriguing—new people to meet, new hands to shake—but Maureen was obviously still not convinced. Still, she agreed to give it a try. I'll tell you the end of this story shortly…

Everyone has moved, and for the corporate nomad, relocating may be nearly as familiar as starting up a new project. Perhaps you've got moving down to a seamless transition and can't think of a good reason to read about it—not when you've got so much else to take care of with the move so close at hand. However, I urge you to read this section, since it provides you with practical suggestions regarding how to use the relocation experience as a business-growing (and comfort-zone-stretching) exercise with your team. The challenges that arise from a change of this magnitude and the ways in which your staff members respond will continue to yield valuable information for and about your business and your team long after everyone has settled in.

The Big Move

Now your team members have been identified and are presumably doing the things that must be done before such a life change occurs: telling children, redefining relationships, closing community involvement, and handling a thousand other details. They're sorting through their possessions, trying to decide what personal belongings they can't live without (funny how suddenly everything seems essential, or holds an important memory). And if you're moving people to multiple locations throughout the region instead of to one central location, which is common given the region's geographic size, you can magnify the complexity of my comments. Meanwhile, over in Asia-Pacific, housing has been selected, equipment has arrived, and the office is quiet for the final few hours as it awaits the team's arrival. The only thing left to do may seem strangely anticlimactic after all the months of preparation. It's moving day.

Preparations for the Big Move

It may seem that never-ending preparations are required when one plans to move to another continent for an extended period of time. In fact, the preparations can be overwhelming. But the key to making the move work—and the key to any potential logistical nightmare—lies in the degree of organization of both individual team members and, of course, the corporation. A well-plotted moving plan should bear a resemblance to a strong business plan, and you'll find that your team members may feel more comfortable preparing if they think of the upcoming changes in such cut-and-dried, measurable terms.

For both physical and psychological reasons, it is essential to be both physically and psychologically prepared for the move. Most of us feel less of a sense of control when we are constantly surprised by unexpected details, you can significantly reduce that stress by creating a clear corporate plan to help your team members prepare and execute their move.

In this section, I want to emphasize the psychological elements of a move. These elements may, at first glance, seem self-indulgent or "soft." You are, after all, part of a corporation, and you're in the business of making money, not in the business of making everybody feel good. If someone feels good, that's fine, but it's probably not in the mission statement. For this reason, many businesspersons would argue that if someone is going to have a bunch of psychological problems over moving, it really shouldn't be up to the corporation to deal with it. Maybe it should, maybe it shouldn't. I happen to believe it should.

What I know, though, is that "shoulds" often fly right in the face of reality. What should be and what is aren't always in the same hemisphere. Read on, but for now, I want to say that regardless of what should be true, psychological issues can make themselves known in the most physical of ways, so focusing on moving vans and sofa placement to the exclusion of whether an employee wants to live halfway across the world will likely result in a move—and long-term start-up effort—plagued with substantial problems.

Let's begin with the psychological issues that may arise while preparing for moving day, since you're not going anywhere as a corporation—not really—until these concerns are addressed.

The Psychology of Change

I've asked this question of a number of people, and the answers I get are always interesting. Try it out on yourself: What's the first issue a person needs to deal with when a big work-related move is being contemplated? Hold onto your answer for a moment, whatever it is. I've heard people say that the first issue to deal with is where to live: what street, what neighborhood, what type of house. Others mention finding the best schools, or the recreational opportunities in an area.

Now, think for a moment about your answer. If you're like the vast majority of people of whom I've asked this question, you made an assumption right off the bat, that the decision to move was already made. I'm not suggesting that no one puts any thought into this decision, just that we tend to make it fairly rapidly, and we tend to look at the physical and practical aspects of a move—such as housing and schools and the like—with much greater attention than we pay to the psychological aspects of a move. If you don't think through the possible emotional and relational effects of a big move, however, in a very real sense, the first decision is still lurking. And while it's true that you've made a decision by default, it's really only a decision you've dealt with on a superficial level.

I recommend that you start out with the first question. There will be time for everything else you need to consider in a bit.

To go or not to go?

That is the question.

Making the Decision

A finite number of people can—and must—be involved in the decision-making process regarding whether you should join the start-up adventure. First, of course, you have to be certain that you are willing and able to make such a move. Then you'll want to involve significant others: your spouse, children, family, and friends. Here are some of the questions you'll be glad you asked yourself:

Is it my intention to be with this company for the next two to three years? If you already had your eye on a move to another company, another field, more education, or another region, how would this move impact upon that? Is it fair for you to cost your current company the expenses of moving you and perhaps a family and training you for the new region if you're not going to stick around? If you're the person choosing the team, you'll want to look closely at these same issues and pay attention to cues from employees who have signaled that they don't have a long-term commitment to the company.

How much do I enjoy the work I'm doing with this company? If you don't enjoy your work with the company in your present location, where you're probably surrounded by friends, family, and the familiar, you are unlikely to notice an improvement once you're overseas. In fact, the opposite will occur, because you will be working long hours, and you will be cloistered with colleagues, since you are all new to the region. This means you will have more time to do what you don't enjoy, not less.

How much am I willing to give up on a day-to-day basis? Ever run into a New Yorker living in a small town? Maybe some adapt, but if you grew up in the city that never sleeps, it's going to take some adjusting to the fact that you can't get a burger delivered at 3 A.M., or a Calzone at any hour in that small town. If you're close to your family, how might it be to live on the other side of the world, where email and a weekly phone call replace your Sunday visits? What about friends? If you're single, will it be difficult to be single in a place where the customs are very different? Think through how you spend your day—you might want to keep a log for a week, jotting down how you spend each hour—and then go through your log and think about how each item would be impacted by this sort of move. Can you handle it? As important, do you even want to?

And more: What grades are my children enrolled in at school? How disruptive will it be to move my family now? Are there any special health or education or other issues with my family members that we might not be able to address outside of the United States? How does the family feel about this move?

It's reasonable to expect that your family members might have ambivalent feelings about making this move—and that's at best. Some will be adamantly opposed. Your teenagers are likely to be furious at the idea, while your young children will take on your attitude, so if you're excited and looking forward to the change, your young children will generally feel the same way. Your spouse may also have mixed feelings; it is a lot to ask of anyone that they would give up all that is familiar and move far from home.

You know your family, and you know how best to approach them, but the key is in first working through issues between the adult family members, and then involving the children. From there, the essential ingredients are honesty, a genuine willingness to take into account everyone's feelings and ideas, and, to the extent possible, a non-authoritarian approach to this decision. Try to remind yourself how it might feel if your child came home one day and announced that you had to go live on Sesame Street—and you had absolutely no control over the final decision. How would you react? The other issue has to do with whether health or educational issues are being handled in the United States that cannot, perhaps, be handled as well (or at all) in a new region. Give this serious consideration. Sometimes compromises can be made. For example, if a wife is pregnant and there is a concern about adequate health care, but both adults agree that the move is otherwise a good idea, perhaps she can remain in your home country, or return for the last month of pregnancy. An open-minded, honest, and thoughtful approach to the decision-making will help ensure that no one feels ignored along the way.

I have also seen couples make decisions not to pursue an opportunity based upon perceptions of how things might be in their new location. I recommend getting full information and visiting the location before decisions are made. It is a lot easier to get the information or see for yourself before deciding than it is to convince yourself or your spouse/family members about the real situation after a decision is made.

How might this move impact each of you psychologically and career-wise over the long run? Will this move create possible substantial financial benefits for you? Might this make the temporary difficulty worthwhile since it is likely to guarantee things you want in the future, like a strong stock plan, money for retirement, or overseas management experience that will increase your own stock when you job hunt in the future? Will you have more options in your corporation as a result of this move? Will you be comfortable enough psychologically in your new job and surroundings? Are you adaptable or do you have difficulty with change? If you have difficulty with change, might this opportunity help you to overcome that?

All Aboard!

Once you've made up your mind about making the move—and for our purposes, of course, I'm assuming you'll go—you need to give some thought to several other psychological issues.

Career Centralization

First, you need to consider the centralization of career that will result from making this move. When you are part of a start-up team, particularly one moving into a culture entirely different from your own, your career will take an even more central role than it did previously. This is true even if it previously seemed to be at center stage. You will find yourself at least somewhat isolated from all but a handful of others (and that handful contains your colleagues, reinforcing the centralization of your work life). Additionally, you will find that the intensity of work during the start-up will necessitate long days—stretching into long weeks.

Also, because there is typically so much riding on the success of this start-up, such as a substantial corporate investment, corporate reputation, and individual reputations, the pressure is on and you're likely to have more difficulty "escaping" from work. I can count more than a few sleepless nights, and I can also recall periods of time when I thought about our operations from the moment I awoke until I finally fell asleep at night—with the occasional work-related dream thrown in for good measure. This can be wearing physically, but it is also mentally and psychologically exhausting. While everyone needs a psychological break, they're hard to come by in the early phase of a start-up.

I recommend several methods for handling the psychological stress of the centralization of your career.

Recognize that this is a self-limiting stage. Eventually, you will complete the early phase of the start-up and everyone will settle in and everything will settle down. I've found it helpful in dealing with pressure if I'm confident that the pressure is not endless. If I can be relatively certain that there's a light at the end of the tunnel, at least in the form of a time by which the pressure will be substantially reduced, it's much easier to deal with it.

Build in escape valves for yourself—and, if your family is there, for your family. This means getting away, but don't use a narrow definition of getting away or you may not ever arrive at any destination. In the earliest phase of the start-up, it may be impossible to actually take a trip that is not related to work. Instead, you may have to "get away" by turning off the phone for the evening and playing Candyland thirty times with your four-year-old (and letting her win). While this hardly qualifies as a break for you, the resulting family peace will make a difference in the overall stress level, and remember, your children didn't come up with this idea to move across the world. They need some degree of constancy maintained. For you, the early getaway may still involve turning off the phone, but then you'll read a good novel (no business books—except this one!), play computer games, or listen to music. Later, as things settle down, work in some actual escapes, trips to Bali, Phuket, Cebu, the Great Barrier Reef, the Great Wall, and other great destinations in Asia-Pacific. Getting out will broaden your perspectives, personally and professionally. What you do is of far less importance than that you do it.

Take it easy on yourself. In other words, tempers may flare, and the pressures of this move may at times cause you to become someone you'd rather not think of yourself as being. Try to take this in stride—it happens to everyone—without overindulging it. Stress and pressure obviously can't be an excuse for acting reprehensibly. The same holds true for anyone who is along for the ride; it is important to recognize that they are experiencing stress and pressure, and to perhaps let the occasional outburst or snide comment pass.

Keep your balance. Despite the fact that your career will become centralized to an unusual extent for a while, it's important not to forget that you have multiple roles (worker, yes, but also spouse? parent? volunteer literacy tutor? gourmet cook? writer? trombone player?). And while you may be too busy to work them all in right now, you need to remember that you have multiple interests, too. (If you don't have multiple interests, you won't have time to get them during the start-up…but you'll want to do something about this once things ease off a bit.)

You'll find that the satisfaction and opportunities for creativity involved in having various roles more than balances out the pressure these roles can bring, and that hobbies or interests are a wonderful way to concentrate on something other than your life as the Guru of Widgets.

Ask for assistance. This can be difficult to do, but I've found that it helps to have people who can remind me that I'm not just Phil, the Chairman of NetCel360, but that I am also a father, friend, etc. You are not expected to do everything by yourself; you have team members and others who can assist and who need to have the authority to set up and run their specific responsibilities. Also, if you are part of a corporation, I recommend you "raise your hand" when you need assistance in the region. Personally, I have never been much of a hand raiser, but the fact is that had I done more of this in the early stages, it might have reduced some of our timelines.

Relationship Conflict

There are several possible scenarios under which you might be operating when moving day rolls around. You might be single and sometimes or frequently dating. You might be single but in a committed relationship. You might be married, and there may or may not be children. No matter which of these situations you're in, a move of this scope is almost guaranteed to create relationship stress, and as anyone who has ever been in a relationship knows, stress and conflict tend to be connected at the hip.

Having experienced four moves to unfamiliar lands or cities, all with small children, I can vouch for the fact that when you make a change of this sort, it can bring out the very worst—and, fortunately, the very best—in two people. While I'm certainly no relationship expert, I'd like to think that I've learned a bit from my experiences. I've seen what tends to work or fail, so I'll pass on a few ideas about the things that seem to be most helpful in managing the inevitable relationship conflict resulting from a move of this magnitude.

Talk issues out in advance. When you're going to make a change of this size, it makes sense to talk about it with your partner, to try to imagine the obstacles and conflicts that might arise, and to discuss concerns, fears, and other issues either person believes are relevant. Everyone has different styles of communicating, and some people are more comfortable listening than talking, but the important thing here is that both people, using their own style of communicating, convey what's on their mind. If you do this, you'll cut down on the number of unpleasant surprises down the road—if not eliminate them altogether—such as a partner's fear that the schools will be terrible, something you might have already looked into and can reassure him or her about. While speaking concerns aloud will not solve them, it will bring them to the table, and that's the first step in their resolution.

Realize that no one is right and no one is wrong. While you're talking about these issues, it helps to remember that there are no wrongs or rights. If your partner is worried or scared about the move, for instance, you won't score any points—or make any progress—by saying she (or he) shouldn't be. She is, and that's what counts. While you can certainly try to reassure your partner, remember there's a big difference between reassurance and ridicule, and telling someone that his or her feelings are wrong smacks of ridicule, not reassurance.

Make clear agreements—and keep them. So much will be unfamiliar and up in the air during the move you are about to make that it helps to have things you can count on, and you should be able to count on your partner. Instead of making some vague promise to "go away together often" during the start-up, as a way of assuring your partner that you'll still have time away from work, it's important to make a specific agreement. Clarify important points, such as: how often? where to? for how long? what are the chances of it being canceled at the last minute?

Remember the adventure. In the middle of so much work, so much change—nearly drowning in details at times—it can take an extraordinary person to remember that this complex set of changes was, and is, an adventure. Like anyone, I've had plenty of over-tired, overwhelmed moments when I've found it hard to keep this thought in mind. Every now and then, my response to remembering that this is an adventure has been more of a heartfelt growl than a heartfelt suggestion to view this experience as an adventure.

If you and your partner can keep the "move as an adventure" viewpoint active, you'll have a better shot at staying positive when relocating becomes difficult. One of the benefits of a partnership is that one of you may be calm and "up" while the other feels less so. If you're doing this solo, however, that doesn't mean you can't have the same outlook; just enlist friends and colleagues who can help get you back on track if you find yourself in a slump of negativity.

Turn it into a chance to reconnect. At home, you can go days with barely a word exchanged with your spouse. It's not necessarily a sign of problems; it just tends to happen when children become part of the equation, especially when they reach the age during which they have lots of activities. You'll see your spouse in the driveway as one of you heads off to soccer and the other heads off to a Scouts meeting. Perhaps, if you're lucky, you'll have a few dinners together, but even those aren't really about connection, since the kids use it as a chance to test out their new knock-knock jokes and you to work out scheduling details.

When you get to your start-up destination, despite the long hours, you will actually have more time with your spouse and children, almost undoubtedly, than you have had in quite a while. There are none of the usual distractions of home, not at first anyway—no meetings, no clubs, no rehearsals, no endless phone calls from the adolescent's friends or dinners inhaled before the eight-year-old runs out to play. This will change, of course, as your children make friends, but while it lasts, you can be aware of the fact that for this short time you're going to resemble a family again. If only because there won't be anyone else to talk to initially, the kids will talk to you quite a bit.

And you and your partner, whether you have children or not, are going to be handed this opportunity to spend time together again, to work together to solve shared challenges, and to become somewhat insulated from the world, much as you were in the early days of your relationship. Back then it was by choice—in the early days, partners rarely want to be disturbed. Now it's more complicated, but why not use your time together to build or rebuild your relationship? Why not talk?

Laugh (as often as possible). Of all the advice I can give, this is perhaps the most important. You'll have plenty of opportunities to laugh (or curse, or cry) as you make the move into an unfamiliar home in an unfamiliar region, where you are surrounded by people speaking languages you probably don't know who have customs you've never even encountered. You will have plenty of opportunities to both feel and appear foolish. You can play this in one of two ways: You can handle it with aplomb and grace—and that's going to involve laughter—or you can spend a lot of time irritated and irritable, holding it against an entire culture and your partner that things are different here. Figure out why you thought it would be the same—it is, after all, a different continent, so surely you're aware of the humor in an expectation that it would all seem familiar? Laugh at yourself once you've seen the gap between what is and what you expected. And then move on, next issue. To me, the choice between irritation and humor is a no-brainer, and the added benefit of being able to laugh at yourself is that other people will admire you for it.

Isolation

The start-up, then, will result in the centralization of your career as well as the potential for relationship conflict. The other most noticeable psychological issue I've seen associated with a start-up relates to isolation, or good old-fashioned homesickness.

A bit later in the chapter, I address ways in which the head of the start-up team (individually) and/or the corporation (systemically) can respond to this issue, since it is a common problem in relocations to foreign cultures. However, in this section I want to first simply discuss the realities of the isolation that can result from start-up relocations and ways that you, as an individual, regardless of your position within the team, can prepare for and handle isolation yourself.

You probably remember the same thing I do from your Psych 101 class. Stick a human in a room alone for too long and that human becomes something less: The ability to communicate effectively decreases; empathy for other humans spirals downward; cooperation and kindness and complex thought and all of those other perks of being at the top of the animal kingdom start to disappear. The theory, as I recall, relates mostly to the fact that we develop and maintain our self-concept—our view of who we are—through interactions. The result of not having interactions with others, then, or not having enough of them, is that we start to lose sight of ourselves; we stop being able to see exactly who we are. This makes it difficult to know how to behave in any given situation, since our actions spring from our sense of self.

If I see myself as polite, since I hear people say I am, let's say, then, that I'm going to behave politely. If I see myself as a leader, since other people treat me as one and reinforce that self-concept, I'll take a leader's steps—and people will continue to treat me as such. It's a nice spiral effect: I behave a certain way, and I receive reinforcement from others; this reinforcement gives me a clear view of myself, and the clearer the view of myself, the more I behave as expected, and so on.

The problem, of course, is that if you're not getting reinforcement from others, either because others are withholding it or because you're not having enough interaction, your self-concept takes a hit. Even though you thought you knew who you were, the lack of feedback from others throws everything into disarray. The same thing happens when someone retires after a long career in which that person defined himself or herself by the job. Dr. Smith—now just plain Betty Smith—doesn't quite know what to do now that people have stopped asking her opinion on medical problems. And Officer Jones doesn't know how to cope with the fact that no one calls him "Officer" anymore.

During a foreign start-up, this is a complicating obstacle. The people chosen for the start-up team are, most likely, some of the big fish in your corporation—they were chosen, after all, and entrusted with this extremely important mission. On a superficial level, they'll be even bigger fish over in Asia, since you'll be operating from a smaller base, with fewer people. However, this isn't really the basis for comparison, since everyone on the small start-up team is likely to be on equal footing, with the exception of the head of the team. The real "pond" for your big fish will be Asia, and it's a rude shock to realize that no one knows you.

It will be quite some time before any of these big fish run into someone on the sidewalk who envies or admires them. For a month, at least, none of your team members will be in a position to mentor other employees. For one, there won't be that many employees early on; for another, those who are there will be swamped. Besides, they're already experts in their own areas. Most of the ways in which we might typically see ourselves reflected positively in another person's eyes will not be possible during the initial phases of the start-up.

On top of that, there won't even be the simple everyday interactions you're accustomed to: the brief exchange with the counter-help at the deli, the joke traded with the guy at the car wash, the dry cleaner who knows your name and doesn't have to be told that you like your shirts on a hanger, medium starch. We don't notice these things at home because they are frequent and seemingly inconsequential; they become memorable only in their absence.

And then there is the psychological issue: These things are absent, and the combination of these tiny daily occurrences with the missing opportunities to form and shore up self-concept can create and compound a profound sense of isolation.

I've seen the isolation that results during this type of move—and I've experienced it myself. It can serve to make someone stronger, but it can also bring out weaknesses and vulnerabilities if not handled well by the individual and/or those around him or her. The question, then, is how do you handle it well?

Isolation Busters

Accept it. The first element of the way to handle a sense of isolation lies entirely within you. You need to understand, first, that this is a common experience. Second, you need to accept that you are feeling the way you are feeling, and that it doesn't mean you're doing something wrong or that you're weak. You've made huge changes—all at the same time—and it is normal to find that stressful and sometimes difficult to adapt to.

Be prepared. The Boy Scout motto never rings more true than when it comes to uncomfortable psychological issues. I tend to think that emotional problems can give us the worst time when we aren't expecting them, or when we think we're the only one feeling what we feel.

Take comfort. Others have come before you, and others will follow, and each of these people will experience a sense of culture shock and isolation to a greater or lesser extent. This doesn't mean you should be glad they're struggling, of course, just that you have an entire pool of resources made up of people who have been there and done that. These people can give you hints on how to make it through the challenge of isolation and loneliness and culture shock.

Talk about it. While you may not like talking about how you feel, keeping this issue to yourself will complicate things in two ways: It will convince you that you're alone with the isolation and it will further isolate you. Once you do talk about how you feel, others will chime in with empathy and understanding, having been there before. If you're too tough to admit that you have the occasional difficult moment, it may be hard for others to feel any real sense of connection with you. When you see yourself as "above" feelings like loneliness or vulnerability, it makes it difficult for other people to feel they can confide their own occasional weakness to you, since there's a sort of judgment involved in being superhuman.

It's all right to give up the ghost and let your fellow team members know you, even with your occasional frailty or human weakness. You want to exercise some care, of course, about when you bring up these issues. As I pointed out earlier, it's generally not wise to complain down in an organization, so if you're the head honcho, give these issues some thought. As the leader, it's not only acceptable but actually invaluable to let your team members know that you, too, struggled a bit with culture shock. If it's more than a bit of a struggle, though, you'll want to enlist help for yourself: Talk to someone at corporate who has also done a for-eign start-up, colleagues from other industries in the region who have gone through what you are experiencing; confide in family members or friends, or seek professional help, but don't burden your team if you're really struggling. Chances are they already know it—it will probably be apparent—but you need to be able to reassure team members that you're doing what you need to do to deal with the obstacles.

My point? You can apply all the effort in the world to choosing a strong team, putting it in great physical surroundings, and smoothing the transition from practical and physical standpoints—and it's wise to put tremendous energy into these issues—but if you ignore the very real obstacles involved in the psychological side of a start-up, you'll spend all your time putting out staff fires, until one day the flames get out of control and take down the whole start-up.

You cannot ignore the hugely significant realities of the psychology of change, of moving employees and their family members across the world. More than any specific advice I can give you, this one fact—that change requires effort and patience and understanding—will help to determine whether your team members succeed or fail. Keep this in mind, and you'll be ahead of the business curve in every way; forget it, and you can do just that—forget it.

Comfort Zones

Remember Buddy and Maureen, the gregarious handshaker and his then unhappy wife? Well, it wasn't that long after we had our infamous dinner that I ran into Maureen at another dinner, a corporate banquet we were hosting for our customers in the region. We were seated next to each other, and after pleasant greetings, we both scanned the crowd for Buddy. As usual, Buddy was working the room, renewing lifelong friendships he'd had for six months, and, of course, shaking hands. You could hear his booming voice from across the room, and Maureen and

I both laughed at the same time as she shook her head at the way customers broke into huge smiles at the sight of Buddy approaching. Maureen started telling me about the trips they've been taking, the getaways throughout the region, and the new friends they had made. She mentioned that she and Buddy had acquired tastes for a number of different Asian foods. The children, she added, really enjoyed seeing other countries in Asia, and were doing quite well. "This is the best thing that's ever happened to us. Life was getting too predictable, too safe. I'm really grateful for this, and I think Buddy is having the time of his life," she said happily, after confiding quietly that the move had originally been outside of her "comfort zone."

I've thought about Maureen's words a number of times since that dinner. I was grateful that she filled me in on how things had changed, and relieved that the move had worked out so well for all of them. Her comment, though, that the move was outside of her comfort zone, gave me the phrase I'd been hunting for a long time. I'd known that a move of this nature was huge and significant and complex, and I had firsthand knowledge of how it could create complex feelings as a result, but I'd never been quite sure of how to put into words that feeling, the combination of anxiety and adventure, fear and exhilaration.

We humans can get stuck in routines and forget how much is out there to learn and see. It's just easier to stay stuck sometimes. Maureen said it plainly, though, and it's a challenge I put to you: Can you make a temporary move outside of your comfort zone for a wealth of opportunity, learning, and adventure?

Critical Mass

So you're settled into your new digs—both corporate and personal—and the new regional office is up and running. Let's say you've been established in Asia for a few months, the typical time I'd expect it to take for an employee to reach the point I want to discuss now, the point of critical mass.

I'm going to compare critical mass to a story an acquaintance told me about a huge snowstorm that hit the East Coast in January of 1996 while I was, thankfully, already in Asia-Pacific. There was some warning, a short notice over a day or two that a blizzard was likely to come—enough for people to stock up on the milk and toilet paper that everyone always rushes out to buy when snow threatens—and then it began. The person who told me the story lived in a big house with his wife and three sons, ages four months, sixteen months, and six years. The snow itself didn't stop falling for three days, and it was another four days before the street was plowed. If you live in the southern half of the East Coast—Maryland and south—you know how incapable the area is of dealing efficiently with much snow, and this storm dumped maybe two feet. Except for the two adults, no one could leave the house; it was that cold, and the snow was that deep.

Gradually, the walls started to close in, and by the third day, the house seemed measurably smaller. By the fourth and fifth days, the adults were arguing over who got to go out and shovel snow—not who had to, but who got to. By days six and seven…well, let's just say that couples have divorced over far less.

What is an adventure for one day, sort of fun for two days, and even bearable for three days becomes downright crazy-making after a certain point in time. Was it Mae West who said, "I wouldn't even want to do something I like for twenty-four hours"?

What does this have to do with heading an Asia-Pacific start-up? Critical mass, which is what can occur for a certain type of expatriate several weeks or, more likely, several months into the on-site expansion. I want to specify that I'm referring to on-site expansion, because you're not likely to see any significant problems until your team relocates and the initial "high" of the move wears off…and then not until the initial intensity of the start-up has geared down. In the early weeks on site, your team will undoubtedly be too busy to take the time to experience any vague feelings of homesickness, culture shock, or general discomfort at facing the unfamiliar in every direction. In addition, because the early days and weeks are so busy, your team members will spend nearly all their waking hours in the company of other team members, and thus will not actually face the same degree and level of culture shock that will be encountered once things settle down. However, just as you might find with a domestic move, once the initial rush is over, your employee may look around and see little or nothing familiar or comforting—worse, he or she will begin to realize the situation is more than temporary. This is not, of course, to say that one cannot make a foreign city or culture familiar and comfortable; it's just that it will never truly be the same as home.

Obstacles to a Smooth Transition

In this section, I want to talk about several issues related to relocating employees and helping to ease their transition—as well as your own. First I'll discuss some of the most common obstacles to a successful and smooth transition. Then I'll share what I've learned from my own experiences in terms of how you can recognize the warning signs of an employee who is struggling with more than just the usual transition woes. Finally, I'll address several methods for approaching and helping such an employee, from the personal interview and support conference to a more formalized system of providing professional help for the employee.

A note before I begin discussing the obstacles: You don't have to be familiar with any kind of mental-health strategies to be able to ease your employee's transition. You don't even have to be particularly comfortable discussing feelings—although, undeniably, it would help. I want to caution you, though, not to skip this section just because you don't think of yourself as a "warm and fuzzy" kind of person! I'm not a counselor, by training or inclination, and I'm not the touchy-feely type either. Instead of thinking of this as a mental-health issue, which I'll address shortly, look at this from a practical standpoint, through the eyes of a businessperson. Anytime you ignore a problem with an employee, regardless of the type of problem, it has the slight potential of going away. We've all seen it happen this way on occasion. However, this type of resolution usually happens when the surrounding situation changes, when the stressors or people involved shift. That isn't going to happen in transition, of course, where the potential for isolation and culture shock will remain constant. Instead of resolving, the situation is much more likely to get far worse, affecting other employees and causing all sorts of related problems.

Think about what happens when you have a small wound on the body. With simple, effective, prompt intervention and treatment, that wound clears up and there's no scar or remaining damage; you often can't even tell there was a wound to begin with. Situation resolved. When the wound is ignored, however, it gets infected; it festers; it spreads first to the area surrounding it and then to the entire system if left untreated for long enough.

From a practical standpoint, you can't afford to ignore critical mass with even a single employee, because it has the likelihood of affecting not only that one employee but staff, partners, and even customers.

Approach this type of problem one step at a time, just as you would approach any challenge. Break it down into small, manageable pieces, handle each in turn, and above all, make sure your employees know throughout that you are on their side. If you have an employee experiencing a difficult transition, the isolation will be exacerbated if he or she senses or knows that this difficulty is also causing alienation within the transition/expansion team. Treat it matter-of-factly, as something that often occurs (and it does), and your entire expansion team will follow your lead. This acceptance, perhaps more than anything, will go far toward solving the problem. It's generally true that a problem seems worse when we believe we're alone in experiencing the problem. Your matter-of-fact approach, which indicates that the problem was anticipated and is natural, will signal to your team that transition difficulties are normal and surmountable.

We have already discussed ways to identify potential problem employees, people who wanted to be on the team for the wrong reasons or are unlikely to be able to handle the multiple transitions (housing, job, country, family, etc.). Despite that, there is likely to be some discomfort, even for the most carefully selected team members, as the reality of the transition sets in. I've discussed this in more detail earlier in this chapter, but I mention it here because it will be impacted by the type of employee personality with which you're dealing. In addition, you may find that you just misjudged an employee—it happens—and that someone you thought could handle the multiple changes is, in fact, having great difficulty. Rather than berating yourself for the bad call, focus your attention on overcoming the challenge and helping the employee to make the transition work. Two kinds of employees are likely to have difficulties with the transition: problem employees...and everyone else.

The first obstacle you're likely to encounter lies within yourself. Our tendency as leaders is to turn every mistake into a learning opportunity, **to focus on how we could have possibly missed the problem potential** with this particular person. I've certainly wasted energy retracing my steps, an activity that may prove useful later, as you plan for future expansions, but is not something you want to spend time on in the midst of a challenge.

Now, before you judge what I'm saying as wrong, hear me out. The best leaders, in my opinion, do precisely that but they time their analysis well. They don't freeze operations while they go back and figure out where the flaw occurred, at least not unless that's necessary to correct the situation. In this case, it's not. In Chapter Four I will talk about the importance of keeping a journal. This is a good place to examine how you might have better anticipated problems with a certain employee, if, indeed, you could have. When working with your team, however, you're better off letting go of the self-analysis and focusing instead on solving the problem.

The second obstacle I've seen interfere with a smooth transition for employees involves **unrealistic expectations**. While I've encouraged you to look upon this expansion as an adventure, as the exploration of the last frontier, it is also necessary to be realistic with yourself and with employees. Starting up a company overseas is hard, unfamiliar work. Living in a land where the language and culture and food—and that's just the beginning—are different requires a degree of flexibility and openness that stretches us, and sometimes pushes us a bit toward an emotional edge.

Dealing with relocated family members who miss home and extended family is another challenge. In every aspect of life, a transition challenges us. To treat transition only as a grand adventure is to do the experience and yourself a disservice. Later I'll talk about specific suggestions for how you can merge the ideas of the challenge and the adventure, but for now, just keep in mind that you can create the obstacle by painting an inaccurate picture of what the expansion will involve, on all levels.

An obstacle I didn't expect but quickly had to face was perhaps the most complicated one of all. There is a certain kind of person—a hard-charging, renegade corporate type, the business rebel—who sometimes makes it onto an expansion team. You read about the Renegade earlier in this chapter, and you'll remember that I suggested being cautious about whether to include such a person on your team. Let's suppose you decided the benefits outweighed the costs, and there the Renegade is, part of your team. He or she is going to be one of your greatest obstacles to a smooth transition. The Renegade is likely to try to make his or her own rules in your host culture, which isn't going to go over well, I can assure you. Let me give you an example of why this is so potentially damaging to transition and expansion.

The employee who tries to pave his own road through a host country is going to have the potential to do tremendous damage to your efforts at transition. He will likely disturb relationships that are newly forming among team members, between team members and locals, and between you and corporate leadership.

The second type of employee-as-obstacle involves the Escapist. You no doubt recall reading about the type, and you may recall that this personality type may be difficult to assess, but I'd steer away from employees, as I said earlier, in the midst of a fairly new marital breakup or long-term relationship ending, who are having financial problems, or the like. It may work out well, giving them a needed breather, but this expansion isn't about them; it's about your company. While you obviously want to take care of your employees, you don't need someone in the midst of a personal crisis on your expansion team. The stress of living in a new culture is significant on its own; piled on top of existing stress, it can prove too much for some employees.

A third type of obstacle to a smooth transition is a direct result of corporate disorganization. If **the communication lines and chain of command are not clearly established and working within your team and between your team and corporate**, it adds to the sense of isolation team members may be experiencing anyway. Going back to Chapter Two, you'll remember that the results of unclear or disorganized communication are far-reaching, and transition difficulties are just one more way in which communication problems can play out during an expansion.

Countless other obstacles can interfere with a smooth transition, from the seemingly mundane, such as the unavailability of a Taco Supreme, to the seemingly insurmountable and complex, such as the loneliness a single team member may feel living in a small foreign town without any potential romantic partners. The obstacles really do run the gamut from the sublime to the ridiculous, and one of your jobs is running interference along the way. Running interference has two parts: You've got to be able to recognize the warning signs that an employee is having trouble making the transition, and you've got to step in and intervene.

Before we talk about how to recognize a team member in trouble, I want to address a question you may be asking: Why are we spending so much time on "soft" employee issues? The reason is that a majority of your start-up team will probably be part of your initial staff. In addition, they will do the majority of hiring and staffing throughout the organization. If you haven't taken care of the goals, relationships, structure, and overall well-being of your start-up team, you will have more problems throughout your organization as you grow.

Recognizing Transition Problems

I think you're going to realize, as you read this, that you already know how to recognize a team member who is having difficulties. The bottom line is about paying attention. You're going to be busy, perhaps busier than you've ever been, and so you may not be as aware as you would otherwise be of the warning signs, but that's your first job: staying aware, staying conscious of what's going on with your team members. You may not look forward to dealing with emotional issues, but it's impractical not to. If any member of your transition/expansion team falls apart, you've just lost valuable resources, at least over the short term, and you've allowed the whole team structure to be weakened.

Your main job in recognizing signs of impending trouble, then, is to stay aware. In practical terms, this means hearing comments in the office, asking people questions about how the transition is going for them, spending time with your team both inside of and outside of the office, and observing your team members for significant changes in behavior. If you even take this first step, and remain conscious of what is happening with your employees, you've made huge strides in terms of crisis management.

Information Central

Whether it's the water cooler or the coffeemaker, every office has a place where information gets shared—and most offices have a person who knows everything that's going on. It behooves you to be aware enough of office relationships to be privy to this information, whether you choose to be a part of the information exchange or not. You certainly don't want things set up so that it appears that someone is reporting to you behind the backs of your team members, but you can pick up a lot simply by keeping your eyes and ears open.

What are you looking and listening for? Not the normal griping that almost always accompanies change. But when it seems to settle in for one person, resulting in a pessimistic outlook regarding a culture, consider yourself forewarned. When you hear a reticent employee suddenly become voluble with complaints, or when a talkative employee stops talking, take that as a warning. When employees who have often shared social activities comment on the repeated absence of a once active group member, take that as a warning. In short, any substantial change in behavior by a team member should alert you. Does it mean you have a definite problem on your hands? No. Does it mean you should check it out? Yes.

Transition Conferences

Both formally and informally, you're going to want to check in with your team members to ensure the transition is going smoothly. If you do so, you can avert problems early on; if you fail to do so, problems have a way of getting much larger than necessary, and then the intervention required is more time consuming, and there may already be permanent damage.

What I have generally done consists of a series of meetings—again, both formal and informal—beginning prior to the move, and continuing throughout the time in the region as necessary. Early meetings would be with the team member as well as his or her family; I've found that putting a face to my name for family members makes the whole process more personal. Family members begin to realize that I care about their transition—and if I care, Dell cares. That is tremendously reassuring to them.

A second type of meeting would occur between the team member and a representative from Human Resources. While these are typically about logistical issues, the reality is that a number of concerns and fears are addressed informally during these meetings.

I also have found email to be a good vehicle for keeping tabs on how people are doing, especially if they are in a different facility. A simple "How are you doing?" or "Haven't heard from you recently, what's going on?" will often be responded to with a request for help or a call or visit. You can really increase the amount of contact with your team through this medium. I have found that if a team member is silent on email or doesn't respond for a period, something generally needs to be reviewed.

An additional type of transition assistance I've come to use has the executive traveling with me for the first week or two of his or her time in the region. Not only does this provide on-the-job training, of course, it provides multiple opportunities for the team member to ask questions and observe how I handle cultural obstacles and the like.

Finally, I encourage creative learning: family and spouse trips around the region, books on culture, language classes—anything that might help ease the transition.

4

An A to Z Approach

Twenty-Six Basics of Asian Start-Up

A: Angles—Imagine Asia-Pacific as a prism in which the many different angles of a situation provide you with a unique and multifaceted view of business in the region. If you focus on one angle to the exclusion of the rest, you are likely to miss some essential element of a situation. This, in turn, will result in a less than complete approach to start-up. Culture, communication, economics, region, language, the personal priorities of your staff, and a host of other factors will influence the outcome; be sure to give these angles the attention they require.

B: Bring—a suit, your passport, traveler's checks, an SOS Card (for emergency medical air flights; you probably won't need it, but if you do, you'll really need it), computers, phones, and other equipment, but these you can beg, borrow, or buy. If you haven't cultivated patience and a sense of adventure, however, you're going to turn challenges into crises and excitement into fear. Don't leave home without either!

C: Customer Segmentation—In Asia-Pacific there are over three billion people and they are not the same profit pool. It's unwise to view all three billion people as existing in one market segment. I recommend that you not segment your markets, however, in one fell swoop. You can't be everything to everyone, and you can't even come close early on.

Establish yourself and your product first, then begin to use a strategy team focused on customer segmentation; this team should identify the details of how to match investment and resources to profit pools.

D: Delete—Get rid of Western paradigms, prejudices, and priorities. In other words, when you leave the Western world and enter the Asia Pacific, you're entering a whole new world. The Western way (personal interests over business interests, preconceived notions, informal chains of command, the propensity to categorize, and so on) is inappropriate and unproductive in the Asia-Pacific. Open your eyes and your mind and start on a fresh page, deleting the old along the way.

E: Ethical Business—In Asia-Pacific, running an ethical business is as much about relationship as anything else. If you conduct yourself and your business with moral and ethical correctness, you will see business success much sooner and you will receive a payoff time and again in terms of repeat business and satisfied customers. How do you conduct an ethical, relationship-based business? Make sure to pay attention to the following:

- *Give first rather than wait for your hosts to give to you*
- *Establish good relationships as the foundation for business*
- *View the prisms in your relationships with vendors/customers*
- *Understand that what is not said is often the more powerful message*
- *Hire great talent so you can consistently meet needs*
- *Go the distance for your customers: in every way, all of the time*
- *Resolve customer dissatisfaction quickly and thoroughly*

~~~~~~

Cultural Note: A Few Words on Lies

Regrettably, there are places where lies are woven into the very fabric of a culture. Asia-Pacific is not such a place. Keep in mind the points I made earlier regarding culture. The Eastern cultures are relationship based to a large extent, and have an ancient and established history built on a foundation of honor. I can't say that I've ever done business in a place where lying seemed to pay off, but at the same time, I think it's important to emphasize the fact that in Asia-Pacific, the consequences of lying seem to be more severe than in some cultures. Of course, it is sometimes difficult to recognize when a lie is being told, and other people may blur the lines between the truth and lies. You know the difference, however; you can distinguish a lie from the truth.

There are several kinds of lies, and often you'll hear people make distinctions, saying a "white lie" is acceptable while another, more blatant untruth is not. I disagree. I see a lie as a lie, and believe any lie rocks the foundation of trust, regardless of the name given to the lie. In a business culture where honor and relationships are so interwoven and so prominent, lying takes on more meaning and more consequence. Whether the lie is one of omission, in which essential information, let's say, is not mentioned, or one of commission, in which a blatant untruth is told, the moment the lie's recipient receives it is the moment in which irreparable damage takes place. My advice? Tell the truth, no matter how hard, how unpleasant, or how much you think the consequences might hurt you. There are no good long-term consequences to a lie. Ultimately, the truth—as the saying goes—will set you free. Put half the energy that lying takes into telling the truth, and you'll be in great shape.

~~~~~~

F: Focus—The two things I want you to focus on when you're involved in a start-up are, at first glance, mutually exclusive. I'd have you focus inward, closing yourself off from distractions, becoming a hermit, of sorts, for the duration, living and breathing your goals for the start-up. Simultaneously, though, I'd have you focus outward, zeroing in on your business plan, on how it will feel to reach success—in other words, on how you'll know you're heading in the right direction—and on your team, reflecting along the way about successes and failures so you can make adjustments during the start-up sooner rather than later.

Recognizing that I have just suggested opposite approaches, I want to address how I think you can focus on both inward and outward experiences at the same time. I think being able to do so is primarily about perception; in other words, if you can allow yourself to recognize that being conscious of what's around you is inextricably connected to what's within you, you'll start to see less of a split between inward and outward focus. Let me give you an example of what I mean.

At one point, in a small, internal meeting, we decided we needed to segment our target customers into sub-markets so our field sales team could fine-tune their approaches—and thus achieve greater productivity. Just after this meeting, word started to leak as we entered the very earliest stages of creating a plan for this segmentation. We didn't yet have a communication plan.

As a result, all of the field troops—nearly everyone who wasn't at the meeting and therefore hadn't gotten the context of the changes we were considering—began to get nervous. Rumors started running rampant, and we even had some managers beginning job searches because the rumors had spun wildly off base, as rumors will. We should have had a communication plan at the ready; change creates anxiety, and a simple plan to address potential changes and reassure staff about the stability of both the company and their jobs would have gone a long way toward stopping the rumor mill. Had we focused on the inward experience—the trust that was still forming, and the anxiety that is such a typical response to change—as well as the outward response, creating and following a communication plan, we'd have all been in better shape.

Consequently, we'd have had less of a split in terms of focus; as it played out, we spent a great deal of energy putting out fires: the anxiety of staff, the distrust from not being informed, the need to create a communication plan in the midst of so much action. We were operating reactively rather than proactively—never a good idea.

You see from my example that it is not only possible to have both an inward and an outward focus, but also preferable and productive. What you're trying to do here is get yourself unfocused on the unimportant or on the things that shouldn't concern you. There may be important details you don't need to deal with; if you micromanage, except in certain critical and select areas, you're going to get bogged down, and the whole start-up effort is going to reflect both your excessive focus in that one area and your lack of focus overall.

G: Guard Against—I'd hate to sound paranoid, and I'm thinking maybe I'm about to do just that with the list I've got going in my head, a list of things I think you need to guard against (is this where I tell you that I swear those people were talking about me?). You know, though, that when you're engaged in a competitive enterprise, it's just reality that you're going to have to watch your back from time to time. What you may not be aware of is that the person you sometimes have to watch out for most is…yourself. Sure, there are always going to be one or two people or firms out there hoping you don't meet with success. It's a reality that by the time you've reached this stage of the game, you're going to have irritated or angered a few people, if only by virtue of your greater success.

That's one thing to look out for, but I'm also assuming that the fact that you're reading this means you're engaged in (or about to be engaged in) a start-up effort, and this means you're doing pretty well for yourself and your company—and this in turn means you've learned how to look out for and deal with less than thrilled competitors.

So, what do you need to look out for within yourself? We can certainly assume you're not a complete screw-up, since you've made it this far, but everyone makes mistakes, and (I believe) everyone occasionally sets himself or herself up for a fall. There's a lot riding on your Asian adventure, so this might not be the best time to test whether your spouse will love you even if you lose your job, or whether your mother really meant it when she said you and your six kids could move in with her if things ever got really bad (and I think we all hope things will never get that bad). Let me tell you the kinds of things I think we all need to guard against.

Regional Naiveté: In other words, allowing the wool to be pulled over our eyes because we haven't done our homework in a certain region, thus making it easy for someone to convince us that there's a 12 percent under-the-table one-time doing-business tax in a given region. If you do your homework, you'll know whether this is the case, and you'll be able to make decisions accordingly. Uninformed is unarmed. If you were asking for a raise, you'd never go into the negotiation without knowing what others in similar positions earn; consider this every bit as personal, and every bit as important.

Titanic Syndrome: Not seeing the bottom of the iceberg is another form of naiveté, perhaps, and it's one that can take you and the whole ship down—and fast. Sometimes we aren't watching closely or we allow others to reassure us that it was just an ice cube, not an iceberg. At other times we don't want to know the depth of a problem; call it denial, call it what you will, but it's your job to keep yourself from being humored or falsely reassured. If you don't acknowledge the scope and possible outcomes related to a problem, odds are that eventually you're going to find yourself ankle-deep in water listening to the violinists bravely play Nearer My God to Thee—-the same song the tuxedo'd quintet played until the bitter end on the Titanic.

What's the answer to this, then? Eyes and ears wide open. A certain amount of skepticism. A healthy dose of I'll-believe-it-when-I-see-it. There's nothing wrong with wanting proof, with examining problems through a worst-case-scenario framework. You don't have to act like a pessimist or take a negative mental approach to problems; I'm simply suggesting you proceed with caution and thoroughness.

The Low Road: Often, there's the easy way, and then there are the other ways. I don't want to suggest that you should never take the easiest path to solving a problem or meeting a problem. Sometimes the easiest path is also the most efficient and the most productive. Other times, however, the easiest path is easiest because it cuts corners and ignores hardships that those who have gone before have learned are necessary for success.

In any business, I think there comes a time when a business ethic gets questioned, when the leader or leaders have to decide what kind of business they're going to run: The kind that does the right thing no matter what, and even when no one's looking, or the kind that wants the fastest buck. I've seen a lot of fast-buck businesses fail, and it's because they get first-time business, which brings early success but no repeat customers. The high road may make for a slower start at the gate, but it generally results in consistency and staying power through the duration of the race. By all means, take the low road—if the low road is the way to meet the needs of both customer and business, and if the low road is the means to the end you're trying to reach, without giving up your business ethics along the way. Otherwise, better to gear up for a longer hike, since that one will get you where you need to go.

Not One of Us: Another thing to guard against is being treated as a foreigner. It's a bit of a bind, since you are, in fact, a foreigner. However, read and reread the sections in this book about culture and about becoming a part of the culture in which you'll be doing business, and read anything else you can get your hands on in that same area. What you want, ideally, is to become an accepted member of the community where you will be doing business. In short, the way to achieve this is all about honor.

Honor, above all, the culture that exists. Honor the fact that your host culture does things certain ways, and your ways aren't necessarily superior. Honor your hosts. Honor the customs of the culture. When you are outside of Asia, you are a foreigner, but once you are doing business and living inside of Asia, be an Asian. By combining both of these into your modus operandi, you can have the best of both worlds.

Surface Judgments: Finally, I want to advise you against making surface-level judgments. In other words, guard against judging things as they appear to be, since things are often very different from how they may seem. This is true regardless of the culture you're in, so it's not going to be a huge change, perhaps, from what you're familiar with. What will be a change is that you'll be trying to merge the concepts of honor and trust, recognizing that those are building blocks in Asia-Pacific, with an occasional X-Files' "trust no one" approach. Don't get me wrong, though; I'm not advising that you not trust anyone. I'm saying that you need to take care not to ignore realities, even when those realities might not be readily apparent. Because I've said that Asia-Pacific contains cultures largely based on an honor system, for instance, you may read into a comment and assume someone is behaving in an honorable, truthful way with you. Don't do so lightly; behave as you would in any situation in which important things are on the line, and find out more. Conversely, you may have had a negative experience with a person from an Asian country; don't make a surface judgment that the next interaction will likewise be negative.

H: Heroes—If someone asked you to define a hero, you might say something like this: a person who saves someone or something, or a person who ignores danger or the chance of harm to himself or herself in order to protect others from harm, or who causes good things to happen to a great number of others, such as a sports hero, and who receives positive acclaim as a result of his or her actions. We could add a number of other points: Heroes get lots of publicity, and often rewards, and heroes are proud of themselves and we're proud of them. All well and good, right?

It may seem like a small thing, but bear with me while I explain. In Asia, a hero is a totally different entity. First of all, there are no self-promoting heroes going around beating their chests and wearing T-shirts proclaiming their names and feats. It just doesn't happen. Second, there are certain heroes known to the whole Asian population, but no subset heroes, people honored by certain portions of the population (for example, while Sammy Sosa was certainly admired by many Americans, he has been elevated to the position of sports hero in the Latino culture since surpassing Roger Marris's record number of home runs in one season.)

In the United States, one is honored and paraded about and given keys to a city after becoming a hero; in Asia-Pacific, being a hero carries with it at least some slight patina of reservation. This may be the result of the more team oriented Asian culture, wherein the individual does not receive acclaim when there is success; instead, it is considered proper to look upon the entire team as responsible for the success. An individual in Asia-Pacific who tries to focus attention to himself or herself will not be viewed positively. Remember, several Asia-Pacific countries are just emerging from regimes in which nonconformity was greeted with raised eyebrows, or even exclusion from polite company. Nonconformity was met, at times, with grave consequences.

The problem with this, obviously, is that Americans are used to the quest for their fifteen minutes of fame, and are accustomed to calling attention to their good works and successes. This can create an immediate chasm between West and East. Your Asian partners may look upon your team members with bafflement or even disgust when the Americans make a typically American move and draw attention to a big sale or a particularly creative solution. Asian corporate life doesn't celebrate self-proclaimed heroes.

Fortunately, it's quite simple to deal with the hero problem; you and your team members simply need to recognize and remember that these differing approaches, which show up frequently in business settings, can both drive a wedge between colleagues and mark your team members as foreigners—two results that can make local colleagues uncomfortable.

But humans are humans, and an Asian worker, like anyone else, is going to seek recognition and reward. That is not the point I am making. What I am saying is that it is one thing for an Asian to seek recognition in a manner accepted within the culture, but another thing altogether to be held up as a hero or star or role model by someone else, especially if that someone else is not a national and doesn't know the subtle Asian approach in this tricky area.

I: Incentives—In Asia-Pacific, substantial differences exist in how incentives are both viewed and managed. I'm going to name and discuss some of the major differences, and then explain why I believe it's important enough to include this item in my A to Z list.

The most essential difference I've observed in terms of incentives is that in the United States, incentives are almost always viewed as tied to compensation. While the occasional corner office or inclusion on a coveted corporate trip or the like can be considered a valuable incentive, the U.S. company offering incentives to acquire or retain a valued employee is typically going to offer money. In Asia, and this goes back to the concept of the relationship basis of the cultures, incentives are only sometimes connected to money. In Asia, a valued employee might be offered the following incentives, all of which would be considered quite valuable.

No-Raise Promotion: The Asian employee will be more likely than an American employee to consider this an incentive, because the job with more importance will change the way the employee views himself and will change the extent to which the employee's family considers him or her successful.

Place of Status: A status location within the office, such as a small office near the senior executive's, would be an incentive as well, as it would indicate that the employee is valued and necessary to the senior executive.

Recognition/Respect: To have a senior-level employee seek out and/or praise a more junior level employee's opinions and ideas is another incentive in Asian business.

Accomplishment: While this category is somewhat vague, to have accomplished something that others have not is also considered an incentive that could be more valuable than small monetary compensations in Asia-Pacific. An example would be Mother Teresa; to be viewed with even a percentage of the affection and admiration that Mother Teresa engendered, and continues to even after her death, would be an incentive far greater than a thousand-dollar check.

Inclusion: Another type of reward is to be included as part of a select advisory or management team, or to be given full access to senior-level executives. These rewards are valuable because they indicate respect, of course, and because they appeal to the strong sense of ownership and inclusion that is both prevalent and encouraged in the Asian business culture.

Given this, I will add that money is still very important in Asian culture. I want to stress that all of the rewards and incentives I mention above are things that can complement or add to financial benefits, whether the financial benefits come through raises, bonuses, stock options, or performance-based incentives and commissions. But it makes sense that in the business setting of a relationship-based culture, incentives of value would be those that emphasize relationship in one way or another, as the above incentives do. In each case, the incentives are about one of two things: Either they acknowledge the importance and value of the relationship between employee and supervisor, or they provide the employee with opportunities for pride with his or her colleagues, friends, and family members. My point, of course, is not to say that U.S. employees find none of these incentives valuable; just watch the maneuvering for corner offices sometime, or the bitter frustration expressed when one employee expresses another's idea as his or her own. I'm saying that these incentives alone are rarely adequate in our business culture.

How, then, does this figure in to your start-up efforts? Quite simply, you need to shift how you view your compensation package. And while telling the bean counters at corporate that raises aren't such a big deal over in the new division in Asia-Pacific won't exactly break their hearts, you're not going to get off that easily. First of all, you have to have incentives, and they're going to be more interpersonal, which—depending on your management style—may mean making huge changes in how you do things. You're going to need to learn to cough up praise and attribution to others for their ideas, or increase the number of instances in which you do. You're going to need to focus on the importance of the relationships and ways in which you can emphasize those relationships. I've spent a fair amount of time discussing how to do so in Chapter 2.

The other thing you're going to have to do is recognize that just because the incentive system hasn't been a compensation-based system of rewards in Asia-Pacific doesn't mean it can't be. You and your company could do your bit to help along the region's economy. In other words, go ahead; tie a bit of compensation to the praise and the soliciting of ideas and the respect you're going to emphasize in your new business setting. (Before you implement an incentive plan, however, research the country's relevant limitations and labor laws.)

I also highly recommend the use of stock options in the early days of start-up. Using stock options has several benefits. First, for the pioneers, I think it creates even more of a sense of buying in and ownership. They directly (and sometimes hugely) benefit from the success that results from the team effort. Second, using stock options is great for morale. It indicates a level of optimism and faith in the company, and also gives every employee who benefits the sense that she or he is considered worthy of the types of benefits that have, in the past, only gone to the highest level of management.

Very few companies consider stock options for more than the top-level managers, but I recommend rethinking that approach. I believe that the top 30 percent or more of employees, in terms of rank, should benefit from stock options, and that an Employee Stock Purchase Program (ESSP) be available to all employees. Even if the number of shares is low, the incentive will go a long way toward creating and maintaining morale.

J: Jokes—I don't know about your approach to business, and if you're still in the planning stages, you may not know yet about your approach to business start-up, but I do know that in business, a sense of humor can save you. This is going to be especially true during an Asian start-up, when you're faced with crisis (or challenge) and change (or growth) and all of the usual business demands that won't stop coming just because you're in the middle of the most challenging experience of your life. In a general sense, then, I think that developing and keeping your hold on a sense of humor is essential, especially during challenges. In a more specific sense, as it relates to starting up a business effort in Asia-Pacific, there are a few things you should know about humor and joking styles in the Asian countries.

Remember that old standby "Just flew in from the coast, and boy are my arms tired…" (ba da boom)? That's just the kind of joke that won't work in Asia-Pacific. While humor—recognizing it when you hear it and having a sense of humor—is important in the region, as it is any-where, it takes a different form than the brassy, in-your-face humor you may have grown used to on U.S. television, in comedy clubs, and the like. For one thing, for the most part, Asia-Pacific has no comedy clubs.

Humor in Asia is not typically about comedy; it's not an act or something that can be written or scripted or presented. It's more subtle, more quirky and situational. You probably know someone who has this type of humor, someone who seems to view the world a bit differently than others, seeing events through a slightly distorted lens and finding the natural humor, so to speak, in situations. This person may not be very good at telling a joke, but his or her one-liners are great because they're immediate responses to situations.

That's the kind of humor you're most likely to encounter in Asia-Pacific. You can probably already see the potential problem here, which is that a frame of reference is essential in order to "get" this type of humor. It depends on nuance, satire, and an understanding of the subtexts of events, and all that is hard-won if you're in a foreign culture.

The good news is that a sense of humor doesn't carry the same weight in Asia-Pacific as it does in the United States. It is not considered such an essential part of a personality. I am by no means suggesting that Asia-Pacific is a humorless society—quite the opposite. It is instead a culture with a bent toward a subtle, contextual type of humor, one an outsider will have a tough time comprehending or attempting. Nor am I suggesting that you subdue or repress your sense of humor. I am saying, instead, that if you find yourself unable to be humorous in ways you might be were you in familiar territory (and you should seriously consider the likelihood of this occurring), it's not necessarily going to result in others forming a negative impression of you. I've discovered that I have to be very conscious of humor, not attempting jokes, for instance, during a speech. If I substitute warm comments and smiles and an open, friendly, nonverbal style, however, I achieve the same goal: direct and comfortable communication between my Asian colleagues or potential business partners and me. I would generally advise against using planned or canned jokes in prepared speeches, and often I would advise against it even in less formalized business settings. The potential for offense is high, since misunderstandings are easy to come by in cross-cultural communication.

I would add just one note on the topic of humor, regarding the potential for misunderstandings and offense: To someone who does not yet understand or know the sometimes subtle differences in cultural features, even the likelihood of a mix-up is hard to gauge. It's like asking someone who has been drinking all evening to tell you (accurately) whether she or he is safe to get behind the wheel of a car and expect that person to make such a judgment reasonably.

I once heard someone (a U.S. businessperson) make an amusing reference, not even a joke, about Buddhism to a group of Muslims, assuming that the two religions were basically identical. To have understood the joke would have required an in-depth understanding of Buddhism, which few members of his audience had. It's not that one can't recover from such a mistake—he did—but why put yourself in that position to begin with? I have actually found that you can have a greater latitude with humor the better your audience knows you, but rest assured that this does not extend beyond a certain point. Always, always avoid religious or other culturally sensitive areas (sexual, racial, gender, and disability-oriented topics would be examples) in humor. They're offensive, not funny…and jokes about these topics are up there with the quickest ways I can imagine for you to find yourself back on a plane heading home.

K: Keep a Journal—I realize you're going to be busy during your start-up effort. Remember, I've both been there and done that. So you may be wondering why I'm coming up with something else for you to do—something that may look suspiciously like busywork at first glance. Hear me out, though, because if I'm including journal-writing in my A to Z list, I'm saying it's one of the twenty-six most important things you can do to ensure the success of your start-up effort.

Just so you don't feel alone (Do you sense a group hug coming on? Don't worry; you're imagining things), I'll tell you that when a terrific executive consultant, Kate Ludeman, first suggested the idea to me, I laughed. Somehow, keeping journals was something I saw as the bailiwick of adolescent girls or people who wear crystals and burn a lot of candles. I am not an adolescent girl, nor am I the candle type. I have always utilized calendars, to-do lists, and goal lists, but never a journal. But I picked up a bound notebook just to jot down details: things I said I'd look into, places I had to stop by to pick something up or drop something off; information I heard that I knew might be useful at some distant date—and that's how it started.

Before long, I'd find myself putting ideas into the notebook, and then the ideas would branch out, with my devil's advocate writing out long lists of the cons and my optimist scrawling down equally long lists of the pros. Before long, the spiral notebook really was a journal, a place where I would record what happened during the day, decisions I'd made, people I'd seen, the outcomes of those meetings—formal or informal—and the like. Now I've been keeping a journal for seven years and I've discovered that it's not only a useful practice, writing all these things down, but it has also covered my corporate back on several occasions. Let me give you an example.

Several years ago I had a conversation with a female employee who had a complaint about being sexually harassed at work. At the time, her words and tone did not indicate to me that she was raising a very serious complaint—just the opposite, in fact—and the employee specified that she did not want any action taken. Despite that, I believed it was important to follow up on the issue, and so I chose to involve our human resources department. They worked with the employee from there, counseling her. We did not hear another word on the subject until almost a year later, when my company was named in a harassment lawsuit—as was I, for a failure to respond. You can imagine how very thankful I was that I had recorded the time and particulars of the complaint and the action taken and the employee's request, as it helped us to resolve the case favorably. I believe the employee and her attorneys were betting that we wouldn't have a clear record of the events that transpired, and had we not, it would have been more difficult for us to resolve the issue in our favor.

Here are some of the things I record in my journal:

Complaints: You probably already follow this cardinal rule of mine, but the journal can help you follow it: Never complain down in an organization. In other words, only complain to your same-level colleagues or to your superiors. Complaining down is most likely going to come back to haunt you.

Take the example of the supervisor, Tom, who bad-mouths a decision made by his boss, Beth. Tom tells his employee, Mark, that Beth is a bully, let's say. When Mark befriends Beth on his way up the ladder, and it gets to the point where Tom and Mark are vying for the same job, do you think Mark is going to keep Tom's opinions of Beth to himself? Maybe, but maybe not. I'd worry.

This is only one of the problems with complaining down; you also run the risk of having those complaints heard by customers, since your frontline people have more customer interaction, frequently, and may not yet have the business savvy to keep the corporate dirty laundry in the laundry room where it belongs. The journal is going to help you follow this practice by serving as a listener when you're all the way across the world in Asia-Pacific, as your only equal on the supervisory chain, when you have more complaints, perhaps, than you ever had back at the home office.

Memory-Enhancement: While I'm sure your memory is just fine, you're going to be dealing in a lot of extra details during a start-up, many of which will be at least somewhat unfamiliar. Your teams will be using project management time lines and punch lists throughout your start-up, but using your journal to keep a running record of what takes place and what needs to take place that you need to pay special attention to is good. You'll have a greater degree of confidence in tracking the progress and remembering the decisions you have made when the details are all there on paper.

Tax Purposes: Expatriates have plenty of things to deal with during the transition, and one that doesn't go away is the issue of taxes. The journal can serve as an important written record of expenses, activities, and the like. We all think we're going to remember every little detail at the moment something occurs (ever decide not to bother writing down how much you took out at the ATM machine only to realize later that you forgot it?). The truth is, there are just too many details to make remembering every one of them very likely. For taxation purposes you will need to record what countries you are in (take my word for it; when you've gone without sleep for twenty-four hours, crossed three or four time zones, had seven meetings in six hours, and forgotten to eat since lunch yesterday, where you were is the last thing on your mind…

Friendship: As the leader, traveling constantly, away from family and home and the familiar, your journal—I know this to be true—can actually serve as a friend at times. You'll read over past challenges that seemed insurmountable when they occurred, and suddenly realize that you not only got through them, you managed them and learned from them, as did your company, then emerged on the other side of the crisis with something to show for it other than battle scars. You're at the beginning or middle of the adventure of a lifetime—but it's awfully hard to see it when you're in it.

Later, reading back, you'll put things in perspective and you'll realize you've made huge strides. An encouragement when you're overwhelmed, a useful if quiet support when you're on your game, the journal is far more than just sheets of paper bound together. Never underestimate the power of words, especially when those words help you gain a sense of your experience and adventure.

Report Card: I also like to use my journal as a report card on customer visits, speeches, presentations, and meetings. I compare the results of the activity to what I had originally planned for in terms of results. The difference between the two, of course, is what you should repeat next time and what you should change next time. It's easy to forget that you can learn not only from others but from yourself.

L: Leadership—How many seminars have you attended that have, at some point, tried to pinpoint a definition for leadership? I think it's a subject of interest and debate because it's so difficult to pin down, so highly individual and perceptual. What you see as leadership may vary drastically from my own vision of it, and yet both of us may be very successful leaders. I define leadership as *"The art of helping others reach a place they wouldn't go by themselves, a place that makes them better than they would otherwise be—both as a result of the journey and the arrival at that new place."* I always emphasize the journey as well as the destination, because the journey is when we learn the lessons and have the experiences that make us grow and improve.

The general idea of being a strong leader is essential whether you're involved in a start-up effort or are in a leadership role back home. I include it in my A to Z list, though, because of the differences between

U.S. and Asian business leadership styles. To ignore these differences is a mistake, a big mistake.

In Asia-Pacific, the leader of an organization is going to resemble a father figure more so than you might be accustomed to seeing. He or she is going to set the tone for the business, and the organization will take on attributes of the person in the leadership position. In a company that already has an established corporate culture, the leader will more likely take on the attributes of the office or the position.

For instance, take the U.S. presidency: It is often said that the office remains unchanged. The person occupying the position of CEO of the country will change every four or eight years, but the basic characteristics of the position—the office itself, and the details attendant upon the office—will remain the same. A start-up, however, whether it takes place in Asia-Pacific or elsewhere, will be infused with the personality of its leader (or leaders). Because there is no existing culture or protocol or precedent, the leader's character and personality will play a large role in shaping the company.

A second difference you may observe in Asian leadership is that the Asian leader is believed—even by the leader—to have more personal responsibility for what occurs within the organization than you may find in the U.S. corporate world. This touches again upon the issue of honor; it is assumed that when one is in a highly responsible position one takes ownership—a sense of personal pride combined with a perception of professional ownership—of what takes place. This is why you might see an Asian government official resign when a frontline government worker makes a mistake that results in a disaster of some sort, such as a loss of life.

Let's say several bus drivers stay up late one night at a retirement party for a fellow staff member; toasts are made, a good time is had by all, and no one arrives home until well past midnight. Early the next day, one of the partygoers falls asleep at the wheel of his bus, seriously injuring passengers. It would not be at all unusual to see a resignation, then, from the Minister of Public Transportation or another executive within the organization, although they were not personally responsible for the act. I don't know whether or not this makes sense to you, but I do know that it seems to create a workplace where ownership—of ideas and of products and, even more important, of the behavior of every other member of the corporate team—is significant, and surely that can't be bad. It certainly beats the "Hey, I just work here" attitude seen so often these days.

There are many types of leaders, and many ways to become a leader, but in the United States, the official leader may not be the person with the true control (that can easily end up in the hands of an emergent leader, someone with a powerful personality and strong leadership skills and ability). In Asia-Pacific, you'll find such a discrepancy to be much more rare. There, the appointed leader is the real leader, typically, and she or he will set the tone for the official and unofficial corporate culture.

A negative leader seems to have less of a negative influence than a positive leader has a positive influence; in other words, I truly look forward to our dealings with companies where the leadership is strong and competent and where that leadership creates a corporate culture of excellence, but I also don't worry about it tremendously when I'm dealing with an organization with a somewhat weaker leader.

My experience has been that the typical Asian organization still maintains the original workplace ethic, to a greater or lesser extent, whether because of or despite the leader. It's part of the Asian cultural ethic to define oneself through work and to assign pride to the work one does, so a weak leader does less damage than she or he might in a culture that does not value worker excellence at every level.

Finally—and this is a last-but-not-least type of issue regarding leadership—I want to state and then emphasize my belief that leadership within Asia-Pacific has to be in the hands of Asians. It is both unfair and unfeasible to expect to put foreigners in positions of leadership in a foreign country on a permanent basis. No matter what the rationale, attempting to enter a host country and take over operations is perceived at some level as carpet-bagging, and it won't work.

We Americans have gotten where we are by virtue of a gutsy, pulling-ourselves-up-by-the-bootstraps, ambitious, visionary, tossing-the-tea-into-the-harbor, the-old-ways-be-damned, entrepreneurial spirit, and that's what makes American business exciting and challenging. That distinctly American approach to business is admirable and much imitated, for good reason. But there is a time and a place for everything, and bringing new business into a region is neither the time nor the place for corporate takeovers, in my opinion. My thoughts on this hearken back to the thoughts I discussed in Chapter 2 regarding the importance of letting one's hosts retain control of the pacing in business. To arrive on the scene one day with plans complete is fine—if those plans are for your organization. To arrive on the scene with ideas for how an established company, say a supplier, should run things implies criticism of how they've been doing things all along, and can be downright offensive and insulting. Get to know their business and them first.

Multinational companies can certainly put expatriates in to start operations and even run them for a while, but they will do the best thing for themselves and for the countries if local leadership is developed over time. In the end, companies should have goals to localize their leaders, as this will provide needed role models for others in the organization, and as local leaders are more attuned to the right angles in the prism reflecting local culture.

As with anything, there are exceptions, but as a general rule, outsiders, no matter how acclimated or assimilated to the host culture, should not be in the highest positions of leadership in that culture over the long run. I have seen companies that still do not have senior management localized, despite being in the region for twenty or more years. That prevents the company from attracting the best locals, as they see the glass ceiling. I think the fact that Asians appear to be barred from the highest level of management and decision-making also contributes to at least some vague sense of distrust or suspicion.

M: Media—This word is important in terms of finances, reputation, and regional presence. You can waste tremendous amounts of money on media and watch your dollars (or yen or whatever) go nowhere, or you can spend small amounts of money, strategically placed, and get huge results. The secret lies in getting to know the region in which you're doing business, and in having a clear, coordinated media plan shaped from the very beginning.

In Asia-Pacific, there are five basic types of media you should incorporate in your start-up. The five types of media, and some suggestions about how to make use of them, are as follows:

Advertising: This, of course, will be more than familiar to you and your public relations and advertising people. All of the usual outlets for getting your product and message across will be available, from print advertising to radio to television to billboards and the Internet.

A few general cautions and comments on media relate to the difficulties inherent in the translation across languages and across areas of expertise. First, make sure your message hasn't been mistranslated. I've heard horror stories, some of which are laughable, although awful, about advertising translation errors.

The example that comes to mind is from a series of ads for a new model of Rolls-Royce being marketed internationally. This worked just fine most places—the very wealthy car-buying public responded favorably to the car and its name: the Rolls-Royce Silver Mist. Unfortunately, the words silver mist carried an altogether different meaning in Malaysia, where the translation related to human waste. As you can imagine, very few people were interested in buying a Rolls with that type of name.

Along the same lines as translation errors are the kinds of errors that can occur when you're dealing with high-tech issues in a complex language situation. I've talked about the latest technology to a newspaper and on reading the article saw that the diagrams and figures they'd used were of a low-tech configuration. We gave them the diagrams to show the progress from low-tech to high-tech, but we had an immediate error in translation just in terms of my explanation of the charts and diagrams.

The single most important thing I can tell you about advertising is that you need to check and double-check when translations are involved—and then check again. You're looking for both technical accuracy (is the correct word being substituted?) and content accuracy (is the process understood? have all the pieces of a plan gotten across?) in translation.

We have had situations where we assumed our ad agency knew what we meant, especially on complex configurations, only to have them presented in an incomprehensible manner to an audience that needed to (and should have been able to) understand. The difficulties were all caused because we did not check the content accuracy. Also, there will be times when you have an important product, idea, or service that may not have a direct translation into a local language. In such a case, you may want to translate it so that it is favorable. If you don't do the translation, the media will, and it might not be a pretty sight.

A few examples that you and I can laugh at—but I'll bet the manufacturers and marketing people associated with these products are still crying:

The Product/Type	How it Translates
Pocari Sweat/Canned beverage	Would you drink canned sweat?
Field of Dreams/Costner Film	I Am a Ghost with Dead Baseball Players in My Cornfield
Puffs Tissues	Streetwalker tissues
Schweppes Tonic Water	Schweppes Toilet Water

I remember when Motorola introduced CT2 phone service as an alternative to cellular service in Asia, and the media translated the name of the service into "poor man's phone." As you can imagine, sales were rough; it took a long time to reposition the technology so sales would increase.

Clearly, it's difficult enough to talk high-tech when all you're trying to bridge are expertise gaps, the kinds of gaps that naturally exist between a computer manufacturer, for instance, and an ad writer or newspaper columnist. It's even worse when you add the complexity of language barriers.

Corporate Relations: I recommend that from the very early stages a public relations plan is devised. Sharing your vision and key messages with the media through interviews, press kits, press releases, company and region backgrounds, speeches, and press conferences can have a tremendous affect on the image of your organization. In fact, if done well, you can get your organization's name and customer benefits out into the public, and this can communicate the air of coporate solidity, stability, and longevity that you want to be communicate to the public.

Investor Relations: I also recommend having a regional investor relations program that is probably a subset of your corporate investor relations plan. Assuming you are entering the region in a start-up mode, you are going to have to set the expectations of the investor community and may even have to educate them as to the subtleties of this region. I have found that the earlier you educate your investors about the region, the better the overall view those investors will have of your company's place in the region.

Employee Communications: Many organizations have done a very good job at the above only to realize they have made more information available externally than they are talking about internally. One outgrowth of the face-to-face forums we discuss is to establish an intranet site where all internal corporate communications and information can be shared among team members. You should make information known internally first, or at least at the same time as externally. This can well save you some embarrassing moments—envision potential customers calling about your new initiative or product and none of your sales or customer service folks having any idea what they are talking about.

These efforts need to be coordinated; they cannot stand alone. Companies that put forth integrated communcation plans receive far greater returns than those that operate reactively or in an unplanned manner. I've seen situations in which a company places a major advertisement about a new product one day, and sees a press conference–generated front-page story about that same product a week or so later in the same publication. Compare this to a front-page story, still generated by a press conference, that runs the same day as that major advertisement for your product. The second situation will invariably generate more leads, and thus better returns.

Branding: You want your company to be the name that comes to mind when a customer needs the type of product you sell or manufacture. It just makes sense. It's important to remember that this won't happen overnight, but you can make it happen more quickly by being decisive about your start-up and by making a strong commitment to moving into a region, identifying the needs of your customer base, and then meeting those needs. Nothing I just said is rocket science, and yet I see companies fail time and again because they don't take opportunities that present themselves; they don't take risks when risks are worth it; they don't learn what they need to know to make a go of things in their new home.

Since you're reading this book, I can assume you're committed to learning, and I hope you'll continue that process. I can also assume that you're responding to an opportunity that faces you, since you're engaged in or considering a start-up. What you need to do now, and this has everything to do with branding, is become the best widgetmaker, bridge builder, computer manufacturer, or french-fry seller—whatever it is you do, become the best. Not one bit less, and considerably more. More than anything else, if you have that as your foundation, and if you follow my next few suggestions, branding will occur more rapidly than you might expect.

Corporate Communications: I think the wisest thing your company can do in terms of preparing for and creating an awareness of the complexities and realities of your start-up is to make a corporate decision to treat corporate communications, public relations, branding, and advertising as you would any other corporate enterprise; in other words, be sure there is a return on your investment. How do you do this? The same way you would if you invested in research, for instance, on a new product: Coordinate efforts between research and marketing and measure outcomes. Don't simply check to see that the article you were interviewed for or the ad you placed made it into the paper. Identify surefire strategies for gauging the amount of business that comes from that article or ad. Give the advertising time to work, but when it doesn't, eliminate that venue. As I discussed in Chapter 2, stay with the publications that have proven themselves to work for you time and again.

A general note on media operations: I've found that the more coordinated the message, the more success it has. If a common theme, such as a tag line, runs in all of your advertising, branding, and corporate communications, whether it's to corporate leaders or individual customers, it will help you to create and maintain a strong corporate presence. Something simple, something catchy, and something "American"—more on this in a moment—will be your best bet.

Some well-known advertising slogans come to mind that illustrate the type of tag line I'm thinking about. See if you can identify the company associated with them. The answers are at the bottom of the page[1], by the way.

---

1. Coca-cola: "It's the Real Thing"; Nike: "Just Do It"; AT&T: "Reach Out and Touch Someone"; G.E.: "We Bring Good Things to Lift"; United Airlines: "Fly the Friendly Skies"

1. It's the Real Thing
2. Just Do It
3. Reach Out and Touch Someone
4. We Bring Good Things to Life
5. Fly the Friendly Skies

Tag lines like these quickly become associated with the companies that create them—-you probably knew all or most of them. You take these tag lines, as your marketing people will tell you, and weave them into every level of advertising. Your print, television, and radio advertising provide the easiest venues, since you either have voice-overs stating the lines or you show them in print. In interviews, you use a more subtle approach, making sure a short, snappy comment—the sound bite—encompasses the idea and, preferably, the actual phrase.

If your tag line is "Yeah, we've got that," (™Staples Office Supply) you emphasize that you're willing to go the distance to meet customer needs, to special order, for instance, and you make it clear that "When we say 'Yeah, we've got that,' it's not an empty phrase. If we don't have it, we'll get it. It's a guarantee." And then, you do it. There are few worse public relations disasters than doing what I recommend--saturating the market with a promise--and failing to deliver. You'll be skewered, and the skewering will be deserved, unfortunately. It is going to be on your brochures, on your corporate baseball caps, on your letterhead, be able to deliver. The idea is to saturate the market so you rapidly and thoroughly develop and deliver on your new business culture.

I mentioned earlier that I'd come back to the idea of an "American" tag line, and I want to explain what I mean. There is, in many foreign cultures, a fascination with all things American. I don't know how deserved this is, but I know it's a reality. Go to Paris and you'll see a café menu offering "le hamburger et les french fries" rather than "le biftec avec les frites." Go to Munich and you'll find a sign pointing you toward "Das Nightclub." While I've advised you to adapt to your host culture, if you're in the process of developing a tag line, this is one area where my earlier advice is not the best bet. Instead, think about finding a distinctly American way of advertising your product or service—something short and catchy, and also something that captures the informal, slightly irreverent, sometimes wry natural exuberance so closely associated with Americans and their culture. Once you've done that, saturate the culture with messages so you develop a presence that is strong and unmistakable. Being the new kid in town doesn't have to mean being an unknown, but your success will depend on your approach.

N: Nonverbal Communication—From experience, some too close to disastrous for comfort, I have learned that what is not said—either because it's hidden away or expressed nonverbally—is every bit as important as what is said—often more so. Numerous communication studies say that when people give conflicting verbal and nonverbal messages, the observers believe the nonverbal messages over 90 percent of the time. More impressive, the observers are correct in their assessments almost 100 percent of the time.

I doubt the results of these studies will come as a surprise; I think most of us, faced with a job candidate who won't make eye contact while explaining that he wasn't fired from his last job, for instance, or with a tearful spouse who insists nothing's wrong, are going to believe the nonverbal behavior over the verbal. It just makes sense.

When you're in a foreign culture, the dissonance between verbal and nonverbal messages becomes even more important to read, since verbal barriers have already entered the communication picture. It's important to be as accurate as possible in as many areas of your communication as possible to avoid the potential for even more misunderstandings than may already be occurring.

Let me give you an example of an incident I recall from my early days in the region. One of our staff members had an administrative assistant resign, and a new assistant was promoted from within. After a relatively short time, the assistant came to me and complained that she wasn't busy enough, saying she had the time and ability to do more but wasn't being permitted to do anything except the most basic of duties, things that had to be done and that she easily accomplished, but nothing else. When she came to me with these complaints, my immediate reaction was to suggest we get her more involved; we were short-staffed anyway, and I was pleased with her initiative and obvious competence.

But it seemed that no matter what we did, she still had the same complaint. I wasn't observing her nonverbal messages closely, though; had I been watching—as I later did—I would have noticed that she shot nasty looks as her predecessor would stop by for lunch with current staff members, and she gritted her teeth when current staff members referred to the way the previous employee had done things. We went back and forth this way, with me ignoring the nonverbal messages while trying to come up with creative new challenges for her, and with her complaining that she still was not challenged. Through a number of sources—confirmed by my own eyes once I started watching—it became clear to me that what was really going on was that the previous assistant still had relationships with some of the other staff members and still met with them socially. The new assistant was frustrated that she did not have these relationships and the same level of closeness; what she really sought was to inherit the total role enjoyed by the outgoing assistant rather than to increase her duties or challenges. Had we identified this early on, we would have saved a lot of time and energy. Instead, we wasted time, money, and effort dealing with false concerns.

Another example I recall was related more to the nonverbals that can cross cultures and then occur between you or your start-up team and representatives of Asian businesses and government.

We were in negotiations with China regarding bringing Dell into the country. The mayor made a prepared statement of endorsement from his superiors, noting that they had supported his decision to bring Dell to his city. What he didn't allude to was the unspoken condition that had been put on that support by his superiors: If Dell did not succeed, the mayor would be considered responsible. His reputation was at stake. Only by doing business in a region—China, in this case—could you come to understand the subtle messages conveyed by equally subtle nonverbal displays. Tone of voice, the pace at which speech occurs, the volume of the words, the nonlinguistic statements (sighs and shrugs are good examples), and so on are all types of nonverbal messages, and they all outweigh the verbal when it comes to believability.

I could share hundreds of similar stories with you, most of which hearken to the point I made early on about the prism: Direct and frank communication like you may be used to is not always the first choice in Asia.

O: Operational Excellence—Perhaps as an excuse for a lack of success, it is often suggested that operations are tougher to carry out in Asia than in other parts of the world. Although I believe some aspects of operations are more difficult, often simply by virtue of being so far from your base of familiarity, some aspects are actually easier to handle in Asia. For example, the very clear chain of command that one is likely to find in Asian business makes it easier. In many cases, to know where to go and who to approach when a decision must be made, U.S. businesses can be much more variable, depending on the personalities involved and the corporate culture.

Instead of putting energy into failure—into identifying weakness in the business culture and searching for difficulties in carrying out operations and obstacles in communication and trade—put energy into success. Reframe difficulty into challenge. It takes far less energy to screw up a business than it does to make one fly, but it also takes more energy to undo damage in the long run. There are self-fulfilling prophecies, beliefs we carry around and then carry out, that can almost assure us of failure, but one can also prophesize success. Make operational excellence your prophecy and watch it happen.

P: Profitability—The time period will vary based upon your goals and investments, but profitability is possible in Asia. We accomplished it in the time period we set as our goal. No excuses. Profitability is somewhat dependent upon the industry you're in, of course, but I've observed that certain industries tend to view Asian expansion as an investment rather than as a return to shareholders, and I think this is a mistake. Viewing Asia as the poor relation is a self-fulfilling prophecy of its own, since you're likely to put less money and fewer resources into the expansion or start-up. The fact is that profitability in Asia-Pacific should not be significantly different in terms of time lines than it would be in any other part of the world.

I've noticed that growth—in income or reputation or corporate presence—is feared and avoided in some businesses. My theory is that it is feared because the business will then have new and higher goals. Some business leaders are content to not move forward as fast as they could, and some fear success. I have found that this is not a set plan; they don't say "I don't want to be successful"; but through their actions or absence of actions, they are indeed saying this. Sometimes it is as subtle as just not wanting to change or rock the boat, or hoping the spotlight never falls upon them; they are more interested in keeping what they have or the status quo. My belief is that you cannot coast in Asia and stay in the same place. If you stop moving forward, you can only coast backward. If you are this type of a leader, or if you are in such a business, better to know this now than to make a half-hearted effort at growth.

If you are not like this—if you're part of a corporate culture that wants to thrive—then you have to behave like it. You can't half-commit or half-attempt anything, no matter how unimportant the detail may seem. Full steam ahead.

Q: Quiet Leadership—We all know a brash leader, one of those loud, backslapping types who is the life of the party—and occasionally the death of an organization, if it's an organization doing start-up in Asia-Pacific. I alluded to this earlier, but the big, loud American won't go over particularly well in most cases in the more socially restrained and graceful Eastern culture. Generally, it's the antithesis of power in Asia to flaunt it or make any kind of show of it.

There are, however, certain situations in which self-promoting, arrogant-sounding displays may be effective. It's not my style at all, but my tone has gotten very loud on a few occasions in town-hall types of meetings when I thought it necessary. The key to not offending was that it was conscious behavior; I was aware of what I was doing and made a choice to switch from my usual quiet style of leadership to the more brash style.

I also think you have to build up to such behavior; if you go blustering into a situation you're going to be less effective than if you're normally restrained and reasonable and then, on the rare occasion when pushed too far, resort to a more aggressive style.

In general, I have not seen loud, brash leaders in Asia-Pacific. More decisions get made in environments of reason and calm than from a bully pulpit. The verbose type may make many people uncomfortable in Asia-Pacific, so you're going to want to tone things down if that's your style. Think about your goals—are they to connect or to intimidate? Are they to cement a business partnership based on trust and familiarity and respect, or are they to make a competitor nervous around you? Rarely, I think, will the second goal in either case give you what you want over the long term. You're going to also want to observe your staff and give feedback to those members who tend to employ the more gregarious, hail-fellow-well-met style.

R: Review Everything—And then, when you're done reviewing everything, review it again. Maybe it will help to visualize it this way: Think of yourself and your organization as one of those Internet weather cameras that never turns off; you're perched atop a building scanning the environment, looking at everything, both up close and at a distance, and even as you're taking in data you're interpreting it. It's an ongoing process that is simultaneously about reception and perception of information.

Your most valuable resource—the one hardest to replace, as you know—is people. So first and foremost, you must be constantly aware of (this means reviewing situations with and remaining responsive to) your team, your staff, your suppliers, your customers, your market, and your organization as a whole. And in your spare time, focus that same level of attention on your family. I say "in your spare time" facetiously, of course, but the problem is that with all those needs to be attended to, the family often ends up getting short shrift. You know this is true, because it's easy for that to be the case even at home, when you're not running a start-up on unfamiliar territory and feeling wholly responsible for its success or failure. Not only does your staff and team need your attention more than usual now, so does your family. And then there's you in there somewhere, with your own bundle of needs, whatever they may be. This combination of needs, the excess of demands and the overload that can result, is something you need to be extremely conscious of and careful about.

Here's the core thing you need to know in terms of keeping an eye on things, and if you follow it religiously, I really believe you're going to be all right: Know yourself, and at all times act in congruence and integrity with who you are. This is reasonable, good advice no matter what you're doing. It will serve you well whether you're playing tennis or leading an Asian start-up (but pay closer attention to it when you're leading an Asian start-up).

The enterprise in which you're engaged involves following a tremendous number of details simultaneously. You must keep a close watch on the progress of your business plan, the situation at corporate, the international financial market, the budding romance between Joe in accounting and Qi in marketing, rumblings from a competitor about moving into the region, the fact that Beth's father is ill back in Virginia and she's having a tough time focusing, a small town's irritation about the factory you want to build nearby their main water source, your daughter's anger at being uprooted from her social network, the beer you've noticed Bill drinking with his lunch...and so on. In other words, pretty much the same things you've got going back home, but multiplied by time and distance and isolation.

So when I suggest that you know yourself, I'm saying I believe you need to have full consciousness about what your beliefs are and about why you're doing what you're doing—why you're in the region, what's in it for you, and what makes it worth it day after day, even on the bad days.

You have to have full consciousness, too, about the commitments you've made to the people around you—both family and colleagues—and your willingness and ability to meet those commitments, even when you are stretched thin. You have to have full consciousness about what's okay with you—what you're willing to accept in your life and in business in terms of truthfulness and respect and competence from others, for instance—and also what's not okay with you. And then, knowing all of those things, you have to make your belief and value system operational, just as you make your business plan operational.

Make sure you live in accordance with all of those things you know to be true about yourself. Just because you're in Singapore, on the other side of the world from corporate, doesn't mean you tolerate the insubordinate behavior of an employee. Sure, it's probably harder to replace him or her when you're not at home, and so maybe you put more effort into counseling and trying to create a change in behavior.

Because of the multiple stressors on him or her in this foreign culture, maybe you are more willing to excuse certain behaviors the first time, or even the second, and maybe you are willing to be more patient than you might have been in another context. There's nothing wrong with that; hopefully you're flexible enough to be inconsistent in those ways—the end result will be a paradoxical type of consistency anyway, but in terms of consistent reasonableness.

S: Scale—This issue is essential, powerful, and omnipresent. But what does it mean? In this context, when I discuss scale I'm talking about creating a single, unifying initiative for your organization so you can move rapidly and purposefully toward profit. It's as simple as that. You start at a certain size or scale, something limited to a certain extent—I've certainly never seen a start-up open in all fifty Asian countries on day one—but pick your goals, prepare, and then make it happen. You need a basic infrastructure in place from the start in order to create a start-up that's manageable and scaled back slightly until operations are full under way. Then, you scale operation costs from there, upping the investments as you watch the return on investments increase; this simple process leads you toward profitability

Too many key initiatives even later in your efforts, but most certainly early on, will keep your troops scattered. Better to keep things simple, with one guiding concept and goal to rally around that is clearly understood by everyone. This will keep staff and customers focused, and will also make access to the goal seem more likely. That likelihood, in turn, will help your team develop and maintain a positive approach, which, in turn, has everything to do with success.

Scale essentially means getting your revenues to grow faster than your costs, and getting your revenues and profits to cover your initial investments. Some organizations like to put all the investment in up front, so that all infrastructure is in place and ready to go at whatever point it becomes needed. This is rarely cost-effective.

If you're building a subdivision, you don't put in the back roads if no one's going to need them for five years. If you're starting up a cellular service, you don't build towers in a rural area where no one lives and no one travels—yet. Maybe in a few years that area will become developed, but why tie up your capital and your staff resources today? Moves of this sort give a company far more capacity than is necessary. You should scale your investment to what is needed now or in the near future and to what your team can absorb.

T: Town Halls—In Chapter Two, I discussed the multilevel approach to communication, wherein you're relying on a combination of telephone, email, face-to-face, and other communication venues with corporate, staff, and customers. In terms of internal communication, I've found over time that these venues are all helpful, but that they are not adequate in and of themselves in terms of getting and keeping employees on the same page during a start-up. Particularly in the sometimes uncertain environment of a foreign start-up, employees want to hear from the leader, and they want direction and information on a frequent basis. Town halls or open employee forums have been a tremendously helpful tool for meeting these goals.

For the first two years, we started every town meeting the same way, with two slides, the first stating our mission and the second stating our key beliefs. The idea, of course, was that we wanted to create and then reinforce a consistent understanding of who we are, and I think it worked. I am aware, of course, that two slides don't create an internalized impression of mission or key beliefs. What really creates that impression is action, but our town meetings were consistent with the mission and beliefs, and by showing that information at the start of each town meeting, we reinforced our message both visually and by our actions.

For starters, we made a decision early on that we'd rather share too much information than not enough. I've always believed that employees have a greater sense of "buy-in" and ownership in an organization in which they have access to not only the information they need but also to the "back story," the information that provides the context for how decisions have been made, for instance. Obviously, certain things remain confidential, but for the most part, our rule was to encourage and then answer questions. In order to support this, we took raised-hand questions, but we also passed out blank cards and made it understood that names were not necessary. Employees asked any number of questions, some embarrassing, and the rule from the start was that any questions would be read, and all questions would be answered. Those that couldn't be answered immediately would receive a response within seven days. We not only made—we kept—that commitment.

Here's an example of how this worked: I remember receiving a question (this was at one of the earliest town meetings) written on a card without a name. The question was a request, actually, for more vacation days. I answered the question in the meeting rather than delaying it, because I knew the answer and also knew we were not willing to change it at that time.

I said that we had decided to subscribe to the national holidays of the country we were in, not adding more, and emphasized that our focus was on scale and adding to the business, and that was where we would continue to concentrate our efforts for the time being—the implication being, of course, that we were not going to focus on increasing generous employee benefits until the organization was strongly rooted in the country and doing well. While it was certainly difficult to say no, as it often can be, the employees respected the direct answer and the way in which the answer fit into those first two slides—the answer was wholly consistent with what Dell was saying all along.

Could I have reasonably deferred this question to human resources? Sure. Could I have said I'd think about it and get back to folks? Yes, that would have been another option. However, to defer a question of this sort can give the impression that someone else is making these decisions or that it is open for negotiation at that moment. I also believe it creates at least a slight sense that you're avoiding something—because, in fact, you are.

Let me put the town meetings in context, because they may not sound like a big deal to you. In Asian business culture, town meetings don't happen. Messages between employee and superior are handled, typically, by courier. While there are formalized exceptions, such as quality circles, the routine transactions of business and the messages that tend to reinforce one's place in the hierarchy do not get dealt with in an open environment like a quality circle. These remain locked in the more formalized courier system, which reinforces the distance between supervisors and employees. The social structure is such that a frontline employee wouldn't think of asking a challenging question of his or her supervisor or an upper-level manager, let alone the president of the organization.

In the earliest days, we met with some resistance, of course, since this was unfamiliar territory for our Asian employees; quickly, however, they became more comfortable with our approach, and I fervently believe that it helped buy-in tremendously.

In terms of logistics, more is better early on. For the first several years, we did the town meetings on a monthly basis; over time I cut back my participation to a quarterly basis and then eventually attended twice a year, as everything was going well. Leadership of the meetings, by the way, was turned over to the respective local leaders

The underlying assumption of town halls is that everyone's participation and ideas are important, and that no employee has too small a voice to be heard. My belief is that a senior staff member has no greater responsibility than to communicate with his or her teams. If the direct communication is left to others, with the occasional memo coming down from above, employee participation will decrease and buy-in will go south. From the front-liners who often know the most buzz about what's happening with customers and out in the industry to mid-level managers who can alert you to internal issues and the like, you have tremendous information resources in your own staff...it's up to you, though, to make use of those resources.

U: **Units**—We probably share a definition for units, but in case we don't, I'm using the term here to refer to product. Those widgets we referred to earlier are your units. My basic formula for success is unlikely to come as a big surprise to you. It goes like this:

Lots Of Units Shipped = Lots Of Bucks Earned

You may not find my formula in any business school's required reading, or at least not in those exact words, but you and I both know that the transfer of units is key to success. Knowing that, remember that business in Asia is done on trust and referrals, so the most difficult time in the start-up is likely to be time spent getting that first account. It will be worth your while to trade off profitability to get the referrals that will inevitably result from the first account, assuming your product and service are good. I think it's easy to underestimate the power of association—association with one local supplier with a good reputation or with one local customer who is known to be choosy about who they get their products from can go a long way toward creating referrals and a niche in the marketplace.

I want to caution you again, though, that this is the stage at which you have to put my earlier advice about profitability on the back burner for a short time. As odd as it may sound, in the early days of a start-up it's very difficult to achieve profitability while you're focusing on profit, since you obviously have to spend money to make money. The lag time between outgo and income may create some discomfort. The fixed costs associated with getting those units out the door have to be incurred long before you ever see any checks in the mailbox. Be prepared for this—it's a basic reality of business start-up. But few people are there at the start-up stage; most of us joined up with organizations that were already well past that stage. I started with Motorola, for instance, and no one was worrying about how to frame the first dollar earned by the time I came along. So even though it's a truism of business we all learned in Accounting 101, the idea of outgo before income is, for practical purposes, unfamiliar to many people.

Here's how I visualize this stage of the game: To get your business to a standing position, you've got to give it two legs—customers and units. Once you acquire those (and that's the slow part of the journey, the preparation and buildup, the courtship, so to speak), life is going to start looking much, much better.

V: Variables—First and most important is a warning: If you cannot deal with variables, with change and flexibility and complexity, do not go to Asia. Having gotten that ominous message out of the way, let me backtrack a bit and tell you why I make such a dire and unequivocal statement.

First, the older I get and the longer I've been in business, the more I've come to believe that everything in life is variable, and life includes business, of course. In Asia, the variables are multi-layered and complex; there are cultural variables as well as variables in language and tradition and business styles and interpersonal styles and any number of other factors far too numerous to list.

In a sense, Asia is not so different from the United States, or from any other country in the world, because it is made up of human beings, and the one thing that joins us all, I believe, is our individuality. We are unique. As a result, no two interactions or businesses or corporate networks will be entirely alike.

There are moments when the knowledge of the variable nature of life can be overwhelming, of course, but for the most part, I find it exhilarating. It wasn't always so for me, and that's why I make the warning I make above:

If you know that you do not have it in you to look upon problems as challenges, or the ability to view complexity as an opportunity to roll with the punches or flex your problem-solving muscles, and if you are genuinely convinced that you never will, you are not the right person to lead a start-up effort in Asia. I state this without judgment. It is far better to know this about yourself and to acknowledge it than to try to bluff your way through the start-up. It won't work, and the damage that can be done to numerous careers and lives is too great. This isn't just about widget sales, not once you've got a team uprooting and moving across the world, with family and Fido along for the adventure.

Do the ethical thing if you're not the right person for the job.

But if you are the right person to lead the start-up, you'll know it because despite the challenges—the countless details and hassles and long hours and stress and strain—you'll feel that sense of exhilaration, too. I've thought at times that the feeling must be similar to what pioneers felt setting out for the West in wagon trains, knowing they were going to face dangers and trials, all for something uncertain, but also for something that held mystery and promise.

If you haven't headed a start-up, don't downplay the pioneering nature of it. Once you've actually gone through the highs and lows, the challenges and the uncertainties and the victories, I believe you'll share my view.

Embrace the sense of exhilaration. The fact that Asia is so variable, that it is, in many ways, the final frontier, layers it with a complexity that will test you in ways you haven't been tested before. In the testing lies the opportunity for you to learn and grow and become more than you are at this moment in time; that is, in large part, a piece of my gratefulness toward the region and its people. Through my experiences there, I have surpassed myself in ways I never anticipated, and I find that liberating and exciting.

At those moments, then, when you find yourself calling the variable nature of the region by another name—unpredictable comes to mind—accept that as real, and find ways to roll with the unpredictability rather than hating it or resisting it.

W: World-Wide Web—Given the fact that many of my years in Asia were spent with Dell, I suppose it's natural that I'd come up with a computer-related term or two in the A to Z section of this book. Of all the computer-related terms I could use, however, the obvious one to me was the World-Wide Web. The reason for this is simple: the Internet, in a few, short years, has revolutionized the way we do business.

In the next Chapter of this book, I discuss the vast changes that have occurred in how we do business in the 1990s. Those changes will just continue to multiply, I believe, and nothing will have a more profound impact on the type and rate of change than the World-Wide Web. From ease of communication to the drastically reduced costs associated with doing business online, the Internet is making us rethink all of the strategies we've applied for many years.

The World-Wide Web is, quite literally, everywhere. It is always available (although some would argue that, depending on the Internet Service Provider!), and it is a treasure trove of information, resources, products, and contacts. It is unlike anything we have ever seen or had before, and the business world will never go back to its pre-Web way of operating. This is a good thing; the Web enriches us tremendously.

In Part Two, I discuss the role and benefits of the World-Wide Web in much greater detail, so I won't repeat that discussion here. The A to Z list serves instead as a highlight of the twenty-six things I most wish I had known, entering the start-up. Of all the things on this list, however, I believe that the Internet is the one with the potential to make your start-up wildly successful. All you have to do is get yourself online, merge onto the information superhighway, and start driving. You'll be on your way.

X: The X Files—You may wonder what I mean by this, but lest you worry that that this twenty-fourth item is going to translate to "Trust No One," a theme on the popular television show, it's not. This concept does, however, occur to me from the same series. **Things are never as they appear,** or so the show suggests. It's probably an overstatement to say that things are never as they appear, but certainly there are variables—those unpredictables we discussed under "V"—you can't anticipate. These can take you under if you let them, or they can simply challenge your ability to roll with the punches.

Let's talk about the serious unpredictables for a moment. War. Civil unrest. An economy that might send any sane businessperson running for the West. Maddening political infrastructures in some provinces or regions. A lack of political leadership or, conversely, too many cooks in the kitchen. And these are all on a good day, I sometimes think.

If you grew up in the United States, you probably don't spend much time worrying about the likelihood of our shores being invaded by foreign armies. You probably don't worry about your elected leader being overthrown. While you may worry about the economy, it probably isn't perched on the edge of imminent disaster as some of the Asian economies have been. To the best of your knowledge, while there's still quid pro quo, direct payoffs aren't a condition of doing business in the United States

Take a deep breath and remember this advice when you're in Asia in the thick of things: Those things (the economy, for instance, and civil unrest) often aren't what they seem to be, and what they might seem to be are signs that Asian culture is ripping at the seams or symptoms that the Asian economy is collapsing. They are symptoms, certainly, but what they are symptoms and signs of is the stage of development of the business infrastructure in Asia-Pacific—in short, growing pains. Any emerging culture and country is going to experience growing pains, and often they'll take the form of unrest and uncertainty. If you'd been hanging around Philadelphia in the mid-seventies (1770s, that is), you'd have seen the same signs from the upstart colonies as they experienced major growing pains and separation anxiety. The economy—if you could even call it that during those long early winters of starvation and illness and hardship—was a disaster. War loomed large. Civil unrest existed between loyalists and the colonists who wanted to break free from Mother England.

My point, of course, is that unrest—economic, civil, political—is not infrequent in a region that is newly forming, and although Asia has an ancient history, of course, Asian business as a part of the high-tech international marketplace does not. The high-tech Western corporate world is a relative newcomer to Asian countries, and it is changing the face of all of Asia-Pacific, from the corporate setting to the world of family and home.

Our natural inclination, I believe, is to try to reduce the complexity around us, or to simplify. We do so by generalizing that which is specific, and by trying to pinpoint the general. When you recognize and accept that things are not always as they appear, however, a requirement is that you give up on any resistance you might have to reality. You accept that the general or vague is just that: general or vague. The specific, no matter how much you'd like to generalize it, is not easily applicable across the board. You accept that variables exist, that the unexpected will happen on a small or grand scale, and often both. You search beneath the surface for what is real, and you recognize that the moment you think you've got reality pinned down, it may well change. Then you get up the next morning and do it all again.

This is a good time to mention something I admire greatly about Asian culture. In Asian countries, age and experience are valued tremendously. In China, for instance, the conventional belief is that wisdom isn't attained until one reaches the seventh decade of life. In the United States, of course, we frequently throw people out of their jobs when they hit fifty-five or sixty. Keep this cultural difference in mind, and know that you are in the process of being filled by wisdom now, by the experiences and acquired knowledge that will lead to wisdom. It's a valuable way to perceive your experiences, and it may help you to keep your perspective to realize that in your host culture you don't have to learn everything today—or even tomorrow—and that you have the time and space to take in the tremendous amount of new information, to step back and begin to understand it over time. It is only after being in the region for a number of years that I have truly internalized this difference, but the relief it affords, and the sense of calm that results in knowing you don't have to figure it all out today, is well worth the wait.

Related to the idea of time and wisdom is a trend or learning curve I've noticed over the time I've spent in Asia-Pacific. While no trend applies to everyone, this seems to be true for many people, and so I want to share it with you. It's what I call the "Three-Year Transplant Curve." In the first year in the region, transplants tend to be excited—that's the predominant emotion and it colors every experience. That's a good thing, because what happens is that the excitement tends to help carry you through the sometimes overwhelming change. In the second year, transplants start to settle in, gaining a sense of familiarity with the region and how things are done, and feeling that wisdom is on its way. In the third year, I've observed many transplants begin to withdraw a bit from the region, and this is frequently when they begin thinking about the next job. Someone who splits off between years two and three, who does not withdraw or begin gearing up for the next adventure, is someone who is committed to the region—and this person is someone to be valued, someone you should focus energy and training and time on, because she or he will serve the organization and the region well. It doesn't happen for everyone, this commitment; in fact, it's more the exception than the rule, but look for it.

Y: Your Sanity—Let's say you've been in Bangkok for a month, maybe two. You've got people counting on you, and the home office doesn't understand what you're going through and your kids hate the new school and your wife is pregnant and scared of delivering a baby in a foreign country and rush hour here makes L.A. traffic look like it's happening on a national holiday and—well, surely you've got the idea by now? It's the "same stuff different day" situation, and if you let yourself lose your sanity over the small stuff, be prepared for it (your sanity) to flee fast.

Your first six months are going to be the toughest, probably. That's the period when the most will be unfamiliar, and it's also likely to be a period, if not the period, when you will be dealing with constant and multiple demands of every type. From a purely practical standpoint, losing your sanity—while it may provide temporary relief—won't do a bit of good for anyone else, or for you over the long haul.

Your key to this early stage is to keep your eyes open and to gather as much information as you can as quickly as you can. Also keep in mind that almost before you know it, you'll be past this challenge, so now is the time to take in the complexities and prepare yourself for the long-term picture, the next two to three years of the start-up.

A word of advice about getting a little help maintaining your sanity: It's easy, sometimes, to exhaust your network if you're using it solely for complaints. Quite frankly, people will tire of hearing your complaints. You've seen this happen, I'm sure; there's always a complainer in our lives, and most of us tend to avoid this person because they're exhausting and they sound like a broken record. Often, I think that complainers don't really want a solution—certainly nothing you suggest is treated as a serious possible answer. Instead, the complaining is more about getting attention or proving the extent of their martyrdom or some other process I don't pretend to understand. You don't want to turn into someone like this, but you do need a way to vent your frustrations.

What's the answer? First, remember what I said about keeping a journal; even if you don't currently believe it will be helpful, give it a try. Second, remember what I said about complaining down in an organization. It's bad business and bad leadership. Third, try to get beneath the surface-level complaints (no good pizza delivery; takes forever to get a copier fixed; the commute costs you three hours a day; etc.) and to figure out what's beneath them. If you can identify the real issues (feeling out of control? out of the corporate loop? isolated? lonely?), you can more easily address them…and then put them away and move on.

Life is different for you in Asia-Pacific, but you are not alone. Others have gone before you and they did not die; others are doing it now. I suggest participating in regional executive groups, groups made up of execs from other industries in the region. You will find a lot of similar challenges, even in different industries. Sometimes it helps to know you are not alone in the challenges you face. Asia also has some of the best resort locations in the world, so when things get tough, take a break, catch your breath, see and enjoy Asia, then get back at it.

Z: Z-Z-Z-Z-z-z-z-z…Sleep. You may think I'm cheating and just couldn't think of another word that begins with "Z" (which is true, actually; the usual Scrabble words like zither or Zamboni don't really seem relevant here, and the only way to make this work was with the z-z-z before sleep). However true, it's also true that you're going to be stretched and pushed and challenged in the start-up, particularly in the earliest months, and that may interfere with your normal patterns of eating and sleeping and relaxing.

If you're a person who can sleep through and in spite of anything, good for you. If worry and stress and change don't interrupt your physical patterns, you'll probably do just fine during this time.

Suppose you're a different kind of person, though. Suppose you're the kind who sits straight up in bed at 3:23 A.M. and says "The banquet on Tuesday! We can't seat Mr. Ling next to Ms. Chan! They can't stand each other!" Suppose you're the kind who tosses and turns, who can't get enough done during the day and stays at the office until midnight and then brings home a bulging briefcase full of more work to do after kissing the sleeping kids and spouse.

A night like that, or even a week of nights like that, isn't likely to do you lasting harm. Most of us have nights like that now and then. In a start-up, though, what is going to happen, if you consider sleep and a normal life disposable, is that you're probably going to let it turn into a habit. Early on, there will always be too much to do. You will never get your work done; count on it. You must develop the ability to temporarily let go of things (overnight, say) at some point, or you will become hopelessly ineffectual. You won't think well, you won't feel well, and you won't function well. You'll get sick more easily. You'll injure yourself more easily. You'll be more likely to snap at people who are also stretched thin. You will also make yourself unavailable to your family at a time when they most need you.

I know these things from experience, remember; in the third week of my first month in the region, I was excited but also overwhelmed. I rapidly came down with an intestinal bug, slammed my hand in a door, and couldn't travel from office to office as needed because my visa was suddenly, inexplicably invalid. When I mention that week to my start-up team, people just roll their eyes and shake their heads; I get the distinct impression that it's better for everyone if we just pretend it never happened.

Although you'll need to be flexible about how much you work—when a crisis occurs, you'll have to stay late and arrive early, of course—make it a general rule that you're going to take care of yourself while you're in Asia. Eat well. Sleep enough. Exercise. Do all of the things your doctor is always trying to get you to do anyway. While everything else is changing, why not throw in these changes, too? It will make a huge difference in how effective you are—and you understand that your effectiveness will make a huge difference in the success of the start-up.

5

Forward Movement

Expansion in the New Millennium

We've talked about culture, customs, and communication. We've discussed the ways to handle the actual start-up from both a technical and a human-relations standpoint, examining the assembly of the start-up team, moving personnel to a new and unfamiliar culture, and dealing with the inevitable obstacles that will arise as a result of the move. In Chapter Four, I summarized a bit of the information from earlier in the book, and presented a number of must-know points about start-up in my A to Z Guide. In many ways, the preceding chapters provide an understanding of the past—the background—that figures into start-up efforts, and the present, or what you need to do now to ready yourself, your company, and your staff for such a big move.

What remains to be discussed is the future. Wherever you're going in the twenty-first century, there are moves that will get you there faster, smarter, richer. I learned those moves in Asia-Pacific, but you can take them anywhere. That's what Chapter Five is all about: the ways to move onward and outward, no matter what your destination, in a business world that is rapidly shrinking because of advances in communication technologies, but at the same time, a world requiring our highest-speed capabilities as managers, workers, entrepreneurs, and visionaries.

In a very real way, back when I was first taking those marching orders and putting the start-up plan in motion in 1994 at Dell, I didn't have the benefit of background, or someone else's experience, from which to learn. Nor did I have a clear picture of what the present needed to involve in terms of preparation. Our team did a great deal of feeling our way in the dark during those initial weeks and months of the start-up. From that experience, I have created this book.

What none of us can know, though—even those of us with the most in-country or in-region experience—is what the future holds. However, the benefit of experience gives me a starting point for focusing on the future, and based on that experience, the following pages address expansion in the new millennium.

The New Millennium

It seems that everyone—government, private enterprise, educational systems, even the average computer-user—has focused on the new millennium as a change-point. While there was tremendous talk about the year 2000 challenges from a technological standpoint (Y2K Bug), there was also an unspoken emphasis on the new millennium as a beginning of sorts. Many people view the first day of every new year as a time to make changes, to rid themselves of excesses and embark on new paths. But never has this human tendency to want to start over, to create a new beginning, seemed more pronounced than it did when people focused on January 1, 2000.

This date, of course, is arbitrary. We could just as easily set tomorrow, or a date in three months or two years, as the change-point. In fact, since you may be reading this at a date later than the opening of the new millennium, you may have already experienced the reality that changes didn't necessarily occur as intended, or the reality that January 1, 2000, wasn't actually so different from December 31, 1999, after all.

The important point to take from all the talk about and focus on the new millennium, I believe—whether it's before or after the change-point—is the natural desire to start anew. That desire is a positive, and it focuses attention on the common personal and corporate goal of creating positive change and growth and forward motion. I want to focus on that goal for a moment as it relates to start-up, and draw from the optimism and positivity such a goal carries with it.

CHANGE-POINTS

There are several reasons why we embrace change. Some of the reasons may not be purely positive; for instance, in the earlier section on selecting a start-up team, I discussed the type of team member who is seeking a start-up position (and its associated change in work, location, and so on) in order to avoid money problems at home, the ending of a relationship, or the like.

Some people may pretend to run toward something, when in reality they are running from something. Others seek change out of a tendency to enjoy the excitement and rush of beginnings—this applies equally, I think, whether you're talking about jobs or relationships; we all know people like this. These same people don't want to do the sometimes difficult, sometimes boring work that comes along after the initial excitement and thrill of the beginning recedes a bit. Undoubtedly, there are plenty of other not-so-positive reasons why people have viewed the new millennium as a time when it would be natural to institute sweeping reforms, to bring forth new programs and products and services—out with the old, in with the new.

Then, of course, there are the positive reasons for creating change, and my experience tells me they may be even more numerous than the negative factors that can sometimes contribute. When I think about the times when I've been behind a change, either instigating it or participating in it (usually both), I can easily identify seven or eight reasons behind it:

- *We seek change to keep ourselves fresh and engaged in what we're doing*
- *We seek change to respond to shifts in technology that require it*
- *We seek change to respond to shifts/needs in the marketplace that require it*
- *We seek change to increase the efficiency/efficacy of our work efforts*
- *We seek change to save or increase financial resources*
- *We seek change to learn about ourselves, others, or issues/processes*
- *We seek change to create a better fit between resources and work product*
- *We seek to bring greater joy or balance into our lives*

STEP ONE: Examining Your Motivation for Change

This is only a partial list of some of the reasons I have sought out change. I include it because I think it's important, before you move onto instituting change, to examine your motivations for it.

I think of the process businesses go through when they create a corporate mission statement and goals and objectives. I've participated in this process more times than I can remember, and I've heard many people—including me, in the past—comment on how painstaking and slow that process can seem. The practical types (again, I include myself) often complain that they don't want to waste time putting words on paper; they want to get moving, do business. I understand this frustration as much as the next person, but I learned to curb my impatience. The process of examining one's goals or motivations (and those of the company) is essential to ensuring an outcome that is in keeping with the mission, the overall reason your company exists in the first place.

In setting up the process for considering and implementing change, then, the first step would be to honestly examine your motivations for that change. Look through my list, and generate a list of your own, since mine is by no means exhaustive. It is also key to recognize if you have even a vague sense that you might be approaching change from the wrong direction—if you're implementing a plan because everyone else has. Just because everyone's doing it doesn't mean it's the right move or direction, it's important to evaluate the efficacy of any change in terms of your own company's mission and goals.

Should you find that your reasons for change are not necessarily the most positive, does this mean you should abandon your plans? No, not necessarily. What it does mean is that you need to slow down and reconsider. Figure out if there are enough balancing positives involved in the change process, and ascertain whether the change you're contemplating will feed into the mission and goals you've set.

Let's assume, though, that you've identified your motivations, and you're certain they're consistent with the direction in which you (and the rest of the company's leaders) want the company to head.

STEP TWO: Worst-Case Scenarios and Perfect Worlds

Once I'm clear about setting change in motion, my next step is typically to start brainstorming about what might happen as a result of the change. You probably do the same thing informally, but I'm suggesting you formalize the process to ensure you don't leave out this step. See it as an essential part of the change-planning process.

You probably also use the term brainstorming to refer to coming up with ideas. That is, of course, what it means, but I learned not too long ago that there's an actual process involved, and since I've started using the "real" brainstorming process, I've noticed an increase in the creativity of my ideas, and a decrease in any hesitancy of staff members in terms of contributing ideas and suggestions. Here's how brainstorming works:

Set out the question, problem, or situation in terms that everyone understands. For instance, maybe you'll say "We're going to brainstorm about the things that might happen if we start making widgets out of plastic instead of metal." That way, everyone involved will have a shared understanding of what's being discussed.

Tell everyone involved that you want them to contribute ideas without regard to whether they're practical, affordable, efficient, silly, brilliant, or anything else of the sort. The point of brainstorming is to remove any evaluation from the idea-seeking stage of the process, so contributors feel comfortable sharing ideas and being creative without worrying about sounding uninformed or stupid—or about currying favor with the higher-ups.

Encourage everyone involved to contribute their ideas, guesses, and opinions about the issue presented. Remind anyone who throws in evaluations that you'll get to that in a bit. It's common, at first, for people to comment on previous ideas. This is the way we all typically share ideas and solve problems, in my experience, but it's not the best way to brainstorm. (It is fine to build on previous ideas, as long as evaluations and/or judgments aren't involved in the process.)

Either with your team or by yourself—and I'd recommend both—go through the brainstorming process to identify the worst-case scenarios of implementing the change you're considering (doing so points out obstacles as well as dangers and also puts success and failure in perspective) and the ways your plan would work out in a perfect world. I particularly enjoy thinking about change in terms of the "perfect world" framework, because what I've discovered is that I can sometimes change surrounding factors about the way the world operates in order to make a change work. Otherwise, I might have just assumed that reality wouldn't support my idea.

Over at our fictional widget corporation, maybe someone makes a brainstorming comment like this: "In a perfect world, we'd make our widgets out of plastic; it would be less expensive and they'd actually break less than the metal widgets with the joints in them." In reality, of course, there was a time when no plastic was stronger than metal. Had someone not opened up to a new way of seeing the world—in other words, had someone not imagined the "perfect world"—creative permission wouldn't have been given to imagine inventing such a plastic—which is currently used in every kind of product you can imagine. The benefit of perfect-world thinking is that it allows us to believe anything is possible.

STEP THREE: Identify and Bring Together Experts

Once you've identified why you're considering making a change and once you've examined the worst-case scenarios and perfect-world perspectives, you'll be leaning toward a decision. It's not necessary to commit to that decision just yet, but it is time to start gathering resources in the shape of experts.

You want to involve a handful of people who have the technical, personnel, management, and other expertise to draw up a comprehensive and realistic game plan. This process should take you a while. In the initial excitement about a new idea, it's a natural inclination to want to make the decision, get the ideas on paper, and use that enthusiasm to carry you through the building phase.

I'm not suggesting you drag your feet—the danger inherent in doing so is that someone else will beat you to the punch, of course—I'm merely suggesting you don't let your enthusiasm overcome common sense. Common sense says it takes a certain amount of time for obstacles to arise, for problems to make themselves known, for conflicts to flare up between ideas and people and the marketplace and your potential service or product.

Once in place, work with your team of "idea people" to get ideas on paper and to explore in more detail what would be involved in implementing the change you're considering. In the pages to come, you'll be reading my five hot tips for expansion in the new millennium, each of which is likely to involve the type of change I'm talking about here.

STEP FOUR: Draw Up a Change Plan

A plan for change is a work plan that outlines the major steps between where you are now and where you want to be. Within each step, your change plan details the actual moves that must occur to reach each of those steps. The more detailed your plan the better, for these reasons:

Detailed steps are easier to assign in terms of personnel. Since they're broken down into small chunks, it will be easier to identify the expertise involved in implementing the step, and you'll be better able to match that need with someone who can meet the need.

Detailed steps are easier to measure in terms of outcome. A step that has even two branches to it cannot be checked off as complete if one branch is incomplete or unsuccessful. This can confuse or slow progress.

Detailed steps provide you with clear, uncontroversial evidence as to where you're encountering resistance or obstacles along the way. It will be easier to adapt or eliminate a small step than it will be to rework one with multiple branches to it.

Future change-planning will be easier if you create detailed plans, since you will be able to use these plans as blueprints for subsequent efforts. You will have clear evidence of what works—and what doesn't—and this will make any future such efforts more efficient. I strongly recommend that after you implement any change plans such as we have discussed, you perform a full review of the entire process and of the outcome. This postmortem will be invaluable in your next change process. Do the same time and time again: What you will find, with each change, is that your outcomes are closer to your goals with each change.

STEP FIVE: Implement the Change Plan

This is probably the step of the change process you're most familiar with and most comfortable with. To be in the position of participating in or leading a start-up, you've undoubtedly been involved in implementing numerous projects and even businesses, perhaps. However, I'd like to make just a few comments, based on my own experience specific to foreign start-ups, regarding implementation of change.

First, I think it's essential to see any work plan or change plan as a work in progress. I called it a blueprint a moment ago, and I think that's a good analogy. When you're building a house from a blueprint, if you discover boulders in the soil just where the well system was going to be located, you don't get dynamite and start blasting out the boulders—I hope you don't, anyway! That's called resisting reality, and people waste tremendous time, energy, and money doing precisely that. If it's on the plans, it has to happen—or that's how the thinking goes.

Instead, if you're viewing your blueprint as a guide rather than as a document etched in stone, you'll move the well a little to the east, where there are no boulders. Similarly, you'll shift your change plan to adapt to reality.

When our widget-makers, who have a work plan specifying green widgets, discover that technology only allows hard plastic to be made in a blue color, they change their work plan to allow for blue widgets—simple. I'm always astounded, though, by the desperation with which people cling to the way things "should" be or are "supposed" to be. While the shoulds and the supposed-to's shake their heads and commiserate about how difficult life is, the winners are moving forward!

Let me underscore that if green widgets are really the only possible solution, you need to find other ways to compensate for this obstacle. Many times I have seen leaders—people identified as such, in any case—spend endless time trying to make a blue widget green, so to speak, when green was never really critical to begin with. If someone had asked the important question early in the process—Is green really critical?—look at the effort that would have been saved!

A second point about implementation of the change plan is that I think you need to be very hands-on during this stage of the process. I suspect it's a natural tendency, once a change gets rolling, to want to take a deep breath and back off a bit, because the whole change process up to this point can be a bit intense. It tends to require some hard work and long hours and continued project management. Of course, continuous changes occur in your organization every day (or will), and you cannot be involved in all of them. Some you will be briefed on; others you will delegate to the team to carry out, with no involvement needed on your part. The changes I refer to above are those critical changes you have identified, the ones that will need your involvement. The implementation stage is the worst possible time to go macro on changes you should be involved in; it's like assuming you're not needed once your kids hit adolescence. You've guided your ideas, like your kids, through the growing years, but when they (the kids or the ideas) first get out on their own, that's when they need you most; it's also when the most problems are likely to occur. Flaws in your plan will become apparent— if you're watching. Benefits you never thought of will also appear, but only, again, if you're looking closely enough to see them.

It will be relatively simple to tweak and adjust and shift things from close up during the implementation stage; what is far more difficult is to go back and try to correct the cumulative effects of obstacles and flaws that weren't caught early on.

Finally, I think you need to try to maintain some degree of objectivity. When you generate an idea—particularly if it happens to be the idea that's going to bring you wealth, vast corporate success, the admiration and envy of colleagues, and so on—it can be difficult to see it clearly, flaws and all. This is part of the role your team fills.

Good leaders know they need at least one person (and preferably an entire team!) close at hand who will always tell them the truth, especially as it pertains to themselves. Being surrounded by yes-men and yes-women is a heady experience, but it's terrible for competence and growth. Without someone telling you what you need to hear about your ideas and your performance, sooner or later you're going to be sunk.

I remember hearing about the young tennis great Boris Becker, who won the Grand Slam in tennis when he was only eighteen or nineteen years old. The first thing Becker did after winning? He fired his coach. Not surprisingly, his tennis-playing career took a downward plunge, but Becker made the mistake many people make when they reach a certain level; they stop being coachable, and they stop allowing anyone around them to point out their weaknesses and flaws. Don't make the same mistake.

By staying open to the possibility that your idea, when all is said and done, may not work—or may not work in its present incarnation—you remain open to the continued likelihood that an idea will come along that will work.

STEP SIX: Evaluate the Change Plan

There are two methods by which I think you should evaluate changes in products, services, or your approach to doing business. First—a point I've already discussed—I think it's essential to do continuous evaluations during any major change, then make adjustments as necessary and keep moving.

I'm not sure I ever really grasped this concept, not in an integrated way, until I heard someone talking about how NASA handles shuttle launches. Despite having thousands of engineers, undoubtedly some of the brightest people in the world, and despite the years of planning that go into any shuttle launch, NASA still makes thousands of corrections, minute by minute and second by second, on any given launch during its initial ascent into orbit. If NASA needs to make corrections on a second-by-second basis, with all of their research, planning, and resources, it seems to me that we all do. What I'm suggesting, then, is that you make adjustments as necessary—and then keep moving.

Second, you need to bring together your team and identify strengths and weaknesses in the change process and in the actual product, service, or business approach once it is up and running and has had a little bit of time to work out the kinks. There are multiple ways to perform evaluations, but my preference is to use an approach that comes at the evaluation from several angles.

Process Evaluations: Ask your experts and team members to participate in both evaluation roundtables and in paper-and-pencil analysis of the process. Your project teams should keep punchlists, meeting notes, flowcharts, budgets, etc.; they are all resources. If your team members have kept journals, this is a great resource for them as they review the steps in the change process and what went wrong—and, of course, what went right.

Self-Evaluations: Ask your team members and experts (and yourself) to evaluate their own role in the process, how they could have been utilized more effectively, areas where they ran into the most obstacles, and similar questions. Remember to pull data and thoughts from your process tools and your journals.

Customer Commentary: Ask your customers, if applicable, to give you feedback on any change. For instance, if the change is that you've started using the Internet for technical assistance to customers, seek out customer complaints, praise, and recommendations.

It may be necessary to offer customers some benefit for giving you this information; a discount, small gift certificate, reduced-rate service, or something of the sort to yield more responses (keep in mind that compensation might yield a more balanced share of responses, since the bulk of survey respondents are typically dissatisfied customers).

Suppliers/Alliance Partners: If your change involves areas that affect your suppliers or alliances, ask for their feedback on the changes you've implemented. You'd be surprised at how willing they will be to share this with you.

These are just a few of the avenues you can use to gain feedback and evaluation of your changes. You are likely to already have additional methods in place for evaluating your existing products and/or services; be sure to consider applying those methods as well to the changes you implement.

On the preceding pages, I've discussed the process that I have used with great success when implementing change in my organization. While this process may seem cumbersome on paper, in reality I have found it to be considerably more efficient and effective than the change processes I have seen in many organizations that are considering and then implementing change.

THE FUTURE OF BUSINESS

So much has changed during the twentieth century. In terms of technology alone, the advances are mind-boggling. Just a hundred years ago, doing a load of laundry meant a washboard and a scrub brush and elbow grease. Catching a ride to the store with someone meant sharing a horse or a buggy.

As I sit here on an airplane, writing this on my Dell notebook, I am completely surrounded by and immersed in technology. Technology waved me through the gate, where I had an electronic ticket; technology is steering the airplane; technology is transferring these thoughts from my fingertips, which would have held a pencil ten years ago, to the hard drive. In many ways, technology will change my life tomorrow and next week and the following week, and I don't even know yet what the changes will be; we can predict what the future of technology holds, but we can't know.

The changes, the leaps forward in knowledge and ability, are happening so fast that many technologies are obsolete the moment they become available, and they're so much a part of our lives that we hardly notice the complexity and incredible brilliance behind them anymore. We take for granted our cell phones, our computers, our televisions, the Internet, our cars and planes and faxes—the list could go on indefinitely. We take for granted the incredible change.

So, where are we going? If we've gone from washboards to motherboards, from the open plains to airplanes, from gramophones to cell phones in just one hundred years, where to now? Those changes already seem like ancient history; we are so accustomed to our technologies—the computers, the phones—that they are taking on the feel of pioneer advances. The changes in the last half of this century have moved so quickly—the Internet comes to mind here—it is nearly impossible to keep current.

Given the rapid nature of the changes taking place in our current world, and the way in which those changes aren't limited to some small corner where the techno-dweebs dwell, how can we prepare ourselves for the new millennium? How can we prepare ourselves not just for the earliest years of the twenty-first century but for all of it? It might be hard to imagine what the future will hold, and that could limit us in terms of how we approach and prepare for the entirety of the new millennium. If we limit ourselves to in-the-box thinking, to linking our ideas only to what has come before rather than to the unimaginable things ahead of us, we limit our future, and that won't serve any of us.

Instead, I want to open up the future by initiating a dialogue about what might be—what could be—if we don't impose the limits of narrow thinking to this process of planning and envisioning possibilities. I have done so by thinking long and hard about the possibilities for our future—in technology, in business, in human relations, and in the interrelationship between all of these things.

What I have arrived at are the five things I expect will still be shifting and growing and changing and taking us into unknown worlds in 2099, just as they are beginning to now, as I write this, in 1999. Read on.

Calling on the Dreamer and the Do-er

The distance between what we think we can do and what we actually can do is often great. This is why there are more than enough clichés to go around on the subject; a cliché is a cliché simply because it is so true. We've all heard that the road to hell is paved with good intentions, and when we start allowing a large distance to come between our actual abilities and our overconfidence about those abilities, our good intentions aren't going to rescue us. It won't matter what you thought you could do when you've just cost the company a couple million bucks. We've also heard another take on the difference between reality and dreams: Those who can't do, teach. These kinds of clichés reflect the reality of the dreamer, the reality that there are those who live with their feet on the ground, their head in the clouds, and, unfortunately, nothing joining the two ends.

And then there is you, right? Aren't you different? This isn't a trick question; no one is watching to trip you up or catch you in a lie. It's a sad fact that reality itself will trip you up if you're going to be tripped up, but otherwise you're safe to dream. Dreaming is what I want to address in this, the last chapter of this book. I don't want to talk about the kind of dreaming I just mentioned, Willy Loman's "Death of a Salesman type" dreaming—the kind where you're always on the verge of the big sale, the big success, slowly watching your life get wished and dreamed away. I want to talk about how to take everything I've discussed up to this point, the thoughts about culture and communication and business and technology—all of it—and integrate it into your dreams, your hopes, your passion. Your passion makes your eyes light up; you could lose yourself in thinking about and talking about and planning for it. Then, once you've merged the earlier thoughts with your passion, I want to give you the five tools you most need to make a go of that passion in the new millennium.

Think back to junior high school science experiments, if you can bear to. Remember the independent variable? In this case, that would be the information on communication and culture and business and technology. Although some people will know more and some less, and how we apply it will differ, the playing field in terms of knowledge is basically level. Everyone has access to the same knowledge base. You also had your *dependent* variable: Here, that's your passion, your desire to learn and grow and succeed. Changes in the outcome of your experiment always depend on that variable, so the more passion you've got, the better your outcome could be assumed to be. That's good, as far as it goes, but I want to take it a step further—a huge step further. That's what this following section is all about; it's about taking you off the playing field, the one that is even for all the competitors, and putting you into a whole different stratosphere. It's going to take a little work—excellence always does—but if you're really sincere about your passion that won't matter. And if you're not sincere about it, you'll know that soon, too.

Let's say you want to build a fire outside. Maybe you want to build a little fire, just your basic marshmallow-browning setup. Or perhaps you're looking to start a bonfire, one of those huge, roaring, powerful fires that lights up a clearing and makes everyone stand back a bit from the heat it puts off.

The information I've discussed in the first section of this book will get you partway to where you want to go; it's the kindling. You've got to have the wood, clearly, but your fire isn't going to burn without at least one other element. What you need, of course, is a match, the thing that ignites the wood, and that match is your passion. When your desire and your passion come in contact with your learning and experience, you become more of a force to be reckoned with; you create an actual outcome—a fire, a business, a new way of doing things. Still, at this point, while you'll have some variance, the playing field is going to remain pretty even, all in all, and it's the same in the business landscape. Your passion to create the best service provider in a region may make your fire or your company burn brighter and faster than a competitor's, but it's still just a fire or a business, not so different from a thousand others.

It's when you look to the environment in which you're trying to build your fire and keep it burning that you'll find the elements that will make your fire burn brighter, faster, hotter. The same is true in leadership and business: When you commit to occupying the leading edge of your industry, to doing what you do better and faster and in creative ways that make full use of available resources, when you decide to stay ready and poised for changes in the business environment and in the world, you will find yourself breaking away from the pack. Because you've anticipated wind, you'll have sheltered your fire so it stays lit. Because you've thought about rain, you'll have developed a way to cover the flames so they aren't extinguished.

While you can never avoid all surprises and shifts in economies, markets, and technologies, you can drastically increase your odds of success. You can merge your knowledge of general business principles and practices and your specific industry with your desire to lead the industry.

Suppose, though, that isn't enough—being an industry leader is a worthwhile position, of course, but it's limited and limiting to only go as far as another business has gone before. Imagine if Mark McGwire had stopped hitting home runs when he reached Roger Maris's record. It just doesn't make sense; you ideally want to build upon success, not stop when you reach its doorstep. If you want more and better, add the tools and tips that follow; make them apply to your industry and to your business, and go forward to lead that industry, certainly, but also to create new technologies, new methodologies, and even new philosophies of how business is done.

When I started NetCel360 with my partner Dennis Smith, our passion for the concept and the technology behind the concept overcame even the conventional wisdom that advised that technology could only be manufactured and sold according to one model—an old, outdated model, in my opinion. That passion was based, in large part, on our belief that the Internet is changing every facet of our lives, and as it does, it is pulling people and businesses into it at an incredible pace.

To me, the knowledge that something that didn't exist, for all practical purposes, six or seven years ago is now so central to how many of us live our lives is compelling and exciting. The Internet is a geographic center; it is a city without walls or borders, crossing all geographic, ethnic, religious, gender, and time differences.

The Internet also puts people in the position of seeing things they would not otherwise be likely to see—and in the moments after we see something new, something that expands us, whether the expansion is shallow or deep, it is a human reaction to want that thing for ourselves, be it material or emotional or intellectual. This, perhaps more than anything else, is how the Internet is changing us on an individual level and thus collectively; it is shrinking the world and erasing one of the stark lines that still remains between the haves and the have-nots, whether educational, social, professional, financial, or otherwise. I believe the hypothetical line in the sand of real or imagined contentment at remaining in one's same position is disappearing—and this will change our world.

In the end, what will separate the winners from the losers, those who surpass the typical and expected from those who run in place, is a merging of passion and purpose. The combination of hopes, dreams, wishes, energy, and excitement—in other words, passion—with organized thought, research, experience, knowledge, and follow-through—purpose—will determine who runs with the big dogs.

It is the human desire to succeed, to surpass those who have come before and to create a standard by which others will be judged; in business, this translates into one that will serve as the model and standard-bearer for start-up efforts and change-planning for years to come.

Do you have the passion and purpose to be at the forefront of the revolution taking place in the world of business today? If your passion is to be a creator and guide in this revolution rather than simply serving as an onlooker or being carried along as a semi-participant, here are the five essential processes I believe will lead to success in the new millennium.

Tip No. 1: Progress

In the mid–1990s—only four or five years ago—a corporate website was not much more than a vanity, a nod to a technology that had not yet truly arrived. The website was almost certainly unseen by all but colleagues and the occasional technology addict, hardly an audience that even earned the site's keep, let alone brought in big business.

Move the clock forward to the present, now, and let me ask you a few questions:

Can you read through any major daily newspaper today that doesn't have an article that makes reference to the Internet?

How many business advertisements have you heard recently in which the business routinely states a Web address in the text of the ad?

When is the last time you picked up a pen and wrote six or seven memos in an hour and sent them off? When is the last time you sent the same number of emails in an hour, responding to questions, complaints, and ideas?

How often do you hear a colleague from another company say, "We don't have email" when you ask for an email address?

In other words, technologies that had not yet been integrated in any substantive way into our lives even a few years ago are now an accepted part of our daily lives—an accepted part of reality. Progress is knocking at industry's door, and it's knocking harder and louder than at any point in history. Progress will gain admittance; the only question is whether you'll be on the inside, welcoming the progress, or outside, resisting it.

More than anything else, what propels the progress knocking at your door is the Internet. Every area of business is impacted by the Internet: communication, purchasing, distribution, tracking of information and merchandise, interfacing with customers, colleagues, and competitors, and accessing the global economy all take place in online. If your business is not yet conducting these activities online, you are probably looking over your shoulder and realizing that you should be. And, in fact, you're right.

There are several key reasons for making a move toward the Internet. Four or five years ago, as I said, we weren't there yet, and at the time many might have argued that conducting business on the Internet was a fad, a passing trend. But it's clear the naysayers were wrong. There are substantial reasons why the Internet didn't go the direction of other fads, and these are the same reasons behind why you should adapt your business and take full advantage of all that the Internet can offer you.

Before I explain why you should be a part of the World Wide Web, I want to mention that I'm aware that some readers might assume I'm biased as a businessperson dealing with the Internet, who founded an e-Business service company. However, this is a chicken-and-egg equation, and that's why I want to address it. I am biased, and I'm not out there looking for ways to burn or throw away time and money, I assure you. I'm in the Internet business for several reasons, but the bottom line is— well, the bottom line! I believe in the power of the Internet and how it is changing business—and our whole world.

That is why I continue to associate myself with the Internet. And because I saw the ways in which the Internet could change how we do business, and because I became aware of the rich potential and the vast, limitless possibilities it offers, I founded NetCel360 along with Dennis Smith. For these same reasons, I am telling you that the Internet is no longer an optional business accessory. The decision to use the Internet has already been made in your industry and in your country. The momentum continues to build across the world. Whether you integrate the Internet into your business—and your business into the Internet— is really only about whether you are going to be a part of business in the twenty-first century. How important is success to your company and industry? To you? What direction are you taking? The Internet is a must-have; it's your company that's optional.

Streamlining Operations

In an incredibly short period of time, the Internet has gone from cool concept to fully integrated into many facets of everyday business. There are reasons for this, reasons that have made this change, more than any other technological advance, move forward at a breakneck speed, and reasons—as I said earlier—that the Internet is here to stay. I want to discuss several of these reasons and the ways in which they will positively impact upon your business.

The barrier to entry into the Internet is very low. From a practical standpoint, the costs are minimal when compared to those of setting up actual "storefronts," a term that can describe not only retail facilities but also all of the related space needs, such as corporate offices, warehouses, and the like. With a core investment for computer hardware, software, telecom connectivity, and some programmers, your business can be up and running on the Internet. If even that sounds too complicated, you can go to one of the thousands of Web hosting firms that will take care of everything for you, and simply pay an annual or monthly fee. You don't even have to set up an information technology department in that case. Every day we see how Internet companies are establishing market niches for themselves or taking on the industry leaders by being fast, versatile, lower cost, and "Internet enabled." Internet-only companies will unseat perennial leaders in some industries if those leaders do not join the revolution, because the value, flexibility, convenience, efficiencies, and momentum of the Internet are just too great.

Customer loyalty only goes so far, and once a competitor's prices drop a certain amount, assuming products or services remain relatively consistent, customers will retain loyalty to savings above anything else. By extending your business on the Internet you cut costs, streamline services, and help assure that your company will stay at the forefront of the industry—regardless of what that industry might be. The Internet will deliver content never seen in one place before. I am talking about information, communications, commerce, entertainment, and services that touch upon every activity in our lives.

Unlocking the World

Until the advent of the Internet, the move from a domestic to an international base could not be made by smaller businesses. Such a move was costly and required substantial other resources—staff hours, expertise, and access to information to start. However, the Internet is like a key to any area, any region in the world doing business. Sitting at your desk, you can research the economy, the competition, the weather trends that will affect shipments, the transportation in an area that will determine whether you can get a needed widget part from south to north efficiently, the income of your potential regional market, and just about anything else you can think of. And, of course, as I suggested above, you can set up shop via the Internet without having to invest the same amount and degree of resources into doing so as you would have to with a physical presence. Now a corporation of a limited number of team members can appear to be a business staffed by hundreds, or even thousands. Your computer serves as the response mechanism for orders, the customer-service desk, and the source for information on your products or services.

Research conducted by Forrester Research in 1999 supports this. In their study, they site that on average a company needed to be at least 1 Bil. US$ in size (revenues) in 1990 to effectively move internationally, and yet they project this number to be less than 10 Mil. US$ by the year 2005. The Internet is the major factor for this dramatic decline.

This is not to suggest you won't want to have actual people accessible to customers and suppliers—more on this later—but rather that you can create a multi-leveled corporation that exists in one motherboard. Add to that the nearly limitless capacities of the Internet and you can take that multileveled corporation on the road, expanding into regions

that are impractical for actual move-ins and consolidating your operations in such a way as to meet the first goal—streamlining operations—
and in such a way as to make multiple expansions affordable.

There is still progress to be made and there are still many processes to
put in place, such as logistics, commerce transactions, and pricing. My
point is that these processes can be carried out, via the Web, in a location different from where you are actually conducting the commerce.
The Web provides you with a potential point of sale on every terminal.

You should be aware, though, that it can also bring the world a little
closer than you may like; in the past, companies could price products
differently in two adjacent countries and not have problems.
Information rarely traveled across these borders. Now, however, your
customers can review your price and service in every country. This
obviously creates a major paradigm shift for old distribution theories.

Marketing to a Segment of One

The idea of marketing to a segment of one is about creating an organizational ethic organized around the customer. You'll notice that I didn't
put an "s" on the end of "customer," and there's a reason for that. It's not
because you won't have more than one customer—we all hope not, anyway—but because I want to encourage you to personalize your business
plan (and the Internet makes this infinitely easier to carry out) for each
person with whom you do business.

There was a time—we see it still in many industries—when progress
was defined by automation. Phones were answered by complex computer menu systems, and still are, of course, and all facets of operations
took place without two human voices ever connecting. This was our
goal. While this certainly can save money and resources, are we sure it's
progress?

I wonder if there isn't a point at which "progress" takes us backward; if you can't get your order problem resolved, for instance, does it really matter if the reason for that is a person or a computer?

We need to be cautious about how we define progress, and recognize that sometimes progress costs a little more and resembles an older, not newer, model, a commonsense model that says what serves the customer best is progress—not what costs least, not what is most expedient, and not what everyone else in the industry is moving toward, at least not necessarily.

Marketing to a segment of one is about superb customer service, and it reinvents the definition of progress based on a more human model of management and industry. Only you will know how best to integrate this into your company, but what I know, and want to caution you about and turn you toward, is that you get to define progress for your company, so don't cut corners. Open up your imagination and your eyes and recognize that what is best for the customer is identical to what is best for your company.

Everything you do in your business should, at a core level, be about the customer. You should ask the following questions:

- *How can we best organize ourselves around our customer?*
- *What are our customer's needs?*
- *How can we best retain our customer? How can we develop true loyalty?*
- *Do we treat different customers differently?*
- *Do we try to create a learning relationship with our customer?*

This connects to your use of the Internet, because the Internet, in significant ways, is very personalized. Ideally your site will be interactive, which will allow your customer to use the site in the way that works best for him or her.

I should note that when I say "customer," I'm often referring to a corporation or to a government client. In fact, when I was at Dell, 85 percent plus of our customers fit into those two groups. Despite that, we viewed them as individual customers, and that's what I urge you to do. As an example, Dell offers personalized Web pages and corporate "Premier" pages for their corporate customers; these pages facilitate procurement, tracking, and customer support. This was how we extended our corporation's "face" to every customer or potential customer with access to the Internet.

Inviting Customers and Suppliers Inside

Another reason the Internet has become so rapidly integrated into the business world, I believe, is because it offers organizations the ability to bring customers and suppliers "inside." In other words, the Internet allows access to ordering, tracking, repair, technical support, and other services in a way that was more difficult when the customer was not at the controls. You may remember the film Field of Dreams and its famous line, "If you build it, they will come." I've found this to be true of the Internet.

If you create a user-friendly, comprehensive website, and let your customers and suppliers know it's there, they will use it. They will also determine what they need from it, which will aid you in continuing to develop your site in terms of what your customer wants. This can become a major enhancement to your existing communications paths.

A potential customer may stumble upon things on your website that they would never have encountered in conversations with sales or technical support folks, for instance. I've gotten reports of this from numerous customers. A website, then, has the added benefit of creating additional sales and opportunities.

How can you bring your customers and suppliers inside your organization? By integrating your communications with customers and suppliers and sharing the information you have. The Web allows cross-sharing of information that only a few years ago would have taken significant investments in Systems Integration development efforts to accomplish. Team with your suppliers, let them know what your customers are saying, what production levels you are running, your inventory levels—and do all of this online. Assuming you have a customer relations plan and a supply-chain-management plan that are individually focused and based on exceptional excellence, you can refocus them for the Web. If your customer model is not up to date or leading edge, with a market-of-one philosophy, it would make sense to recreate it now rather than try to adapt something that already has substantial shortcomings.

Let's assume, though, that your model is already comprehensive and excellent. I think the best bet is to take this model and create parallel methods for meeting its goals on the Internet.

At Dell, for instance, we took our "Direct Model," which I discuss in more detail below, and extended it into the Internet. The Direct Model stresses direct relationships with customers and built-to-order products and services on a global basis. The Internet model of Dell bringing everything they do to the fingertips of their customers was a natural extension of the business model. The innovations that have accompanied this are the result of great folks taking initiative and leading the way. In specific, concrete terms, Web adaptation translates to streamlined customer access to Dell support information: over 35,000 pages of technical reference materials, order status information, and the like. While customers can continue to communicate with their account representative on the phone or in person, they can also access Dell via the Internet—twenty-four hours a day, seven days a week, from anywhere in the world. According to Dell's most recent quarterly report, sales from website are greater than $ 50 million a day, accounting for more than 50 percent of Dell's revenues. Clearly the purchasing public is making good use of Dell's website.

Your first goal in inviting customers and suppliers inside is to make sure the website is welcoming. You wouldn't invite a corporate guest into headquarters and say "Have fun finding the conference room!" and disappear down the hall, would you? You'd lead them to it; you'd offer directions; you'd also make sure that the carpets are kept clean, there's pleasant art on the walls, and so forth. Your website is a virtual office, and it needs to be pleasing in appearance and easy to navigate.

Dell's website, which is designed to be easy to use, can be navigated using different languages throughout the world. In part as a result of this ease of use, Dell receives about 50 percent of its business over the Internet, and has goals to increase this even higher. Adding languages, creating personalized websites, offering customers twenty-four hour shopping and support services, providing full product and technology information, allowing customers to track every step of the way as their computers are built—these are just a few of the ways in which Dell uses the Internet to create a "market of one" in a global economy.

How to Do It

Above, I've discussed why I believe you should create an Internet presence for your business and why I believe the Internet is here to stay. I've also discussed specific recommendations for what you might offer your customers on the Internet. But before you start figuring out your web site layout, you need to give serious consideration to your goals and then your strategies.

I recommend starting out by reviewing the Internet activities in your industry. See what your competitors are doing. You may also find it helpful to see what others outside of your industry are doing on the Internet; many ideas can be adapted from one industry to another. Think about how these activities fit—or don't fit—with the mission and goals of your particular business.

If you review your goals—let's say they include more sales, more earnings, and positive customer ratings of your company—and then decide the Internet won't serve those goals (and frankly, I don't buy it; I'd go back and try to find the missing link if you reach this the conclusion!), you will at least have created a clear policy of non-participation at this time.

I believe very few—if any—industries will not be affected by the Internet in the long run. For that matter, I think very few industries are not already being impacted by the Internet. I speak to senior leaders in various organizations, and am always amazed when there is a blind spot about the Internet—or when the leaders comment that they have not actually even been on the Internet. Here's what I would ask in that case:

- *Do you know what your industry is doing in the Internet?*
- *How will this affect your business?*
- *Do you have an Internet strategy?*
- *If your customers flock to the Internet and demand you have a presence there, what are you going to do?*
- *Has your team reviewed the efficiencies that the Web can bring in your supply-chain management?*

I could continue with a much longer list, but you get the idea. It is my contention that the Internet, and all of the access and options it brings, is not a luxury; it's a necessity and a huge benefit to businesses, governments, institutions, and to the users themselves.

Asia is lagging the US in e-Business development, but it is catching up very fast. In a survey conducted by Goldman Sachs in early 2000, it was reported that over 60% of CEO's surveyed in Asia said that they recognized the need for an e-Business plan only within the last 12 months. Additionally, it was found that 81% of the CEO's said their organizations were either still planning or in the earliest stages of e-Business implementation. The fact that plans are being made and implementation has started holds well for the region, and should make us all aware that the impact of the Internet on business in Asia is still to come!

Review your goals, both corporate wide and on a more daily basis, in terms of customer interactions, sales projections, service delivery, and similar areas, then merge those goals with strategies you create to meet them. The most important strategies are to break your existing paradigms and brainstorm what could be—not what is or what seems easily doable, but what could be. It is when you open your mind to the possible—and the seemingly impossible—that creative change occurs.

Additionally, I recommend that every organization move toward connecting every employee to email, the Internet, and intranet at work, at home, and on the road. You will have to make the decision of how this applies to your business, of course, but if employees are more connected, I'd argue that they will be more responsive to customers—and I can't find anything objectionable about that! That is progress, and to put it plainly, if you're not moving forward, you're sliding backward and losing ground. There is no standing still in business today.

Tip No. 2: Process

Have you ever created a plan for something—a complex plan, let's say, one that took you a lot of time and effort—and then, sometime down the road, the plan needed changes? Maybe your boss handed it to you all marked up, and said there were some basic problems, but that you could keep the guts of the plan—just change everything else. You were frustrated, probably, but you cut and you pasted and you changed this and deleted that and the farther you got into the revisions, the worse the plan looked. In fact, it didn't even resemble the original plan by this point (not necessarily a bad thing), but, unfortunately, it also seemed to get farther away from its intended goals with each change you made. Finally, after hours of trying to revise the document, you gave up...and started an entirely new plan. That one fit the goals. That one came together with ease. That one made it through the review with flying colors.

We've all done it, assuming it would be easier to build on what we've got, whether it's a business plan or the business itself. It seems like a waste of time to start over, reinventing the wheel—but that's sometimes based on faulty logic.

You have to have the wheel to begin with in order to reinvent it.

When I use the word process, I'm talking about the act of reinvention. The path you take toward change and growth will result in revised practices and new processes; if you can't embrace change and growth, those practices and processes will just be more of the same and your company won't thrive in a world demanding excellence. The competition is too fierce, the pace of change too rapid, and the technologies far too fluid and fast growing to allow half-efforts or dull repeat performances.

Your business model—how you've managed your business in the past—may work like a charm in your home country or market. However, this by no means guarantees it's going to work well in your foreign start-up. It may have absolutely no relation to how you will need (or want) to do business in a foreign market; thus, from a practical standpoint, you must examine your goals with objectivity and precision. Review your core competencies. Do they apply in the new market, or are modifications necessary?

There are two levels to the process of growth and change: the art of passion and the science of precision. Ignore either of the two levels—in other words, dream without having a plan of action, or develop a plan of action without passion—and you're just treading water.

I'd go so far as to say that every business would do well, as we enter the new millennium, to review its current business model and determine what changes, enhancements, and extensions would best serve the customer and the corporation. However, if you're embarking on a start-up, I consider a review and redefinition to be nonnegotiable. The way to approach this review and redefinition process is with the passion and practicality I've just mentioned. This is the time to look with your eyes wide open, to examine what has worked in the past for your company and for other companies…and, just as important, what has not worked. And then, having been unerring and truthful in this review, is the time to apply the magic of the creation process to your start-up: Don't replicate a model in Asia that needs to be changed. Change it. Reinvent the wheel, and do it with passion and precision.

If I haven't convinced you of the need to approach the years to come in a way that combines both preparedness and something more intangible—some business ethic made up of passion and pride and the processes that will carry you through change, no matter what that change is—let me say a bit more on being ready for change.

If you saw the original *Austin Powers* movie, you'll remember it was based on one of those absurd concepts: A man had been frozen, suspended in some solution since the late sixties. Brought back to life in the nineties, he experienced culture shock at the changes around him. The movie is a comedy, but the underlying idea illustrates a point I want to make. Unless your company has entered the corporate world very recently, or unless your company has been watching and adjusting and refocusing all the way down the line, you may discover that substantial changes have taken place in how business is done—all while you've been doing business in the same old ways.

For so many businesses, the day-to-day process of crisis management and simply being reactive eat up every bit of person power; there is little, if any, time left for the slow, steady, and thoughtful process work that signals the proactive organization. Being part of a company today, with change occurring so rapidly, at times does resemble the Austin Powers time warp. While the world continues to move and change, it's easy to stay inside reacting, unaware of anything that isn't directly confronting the company. Shifts in business and management—things like the direct model approach, supply-chain management, virtual corporations, intra-industry consolidation, consolidation across industries, and the globalization of industry—are all shifts in the way business is done, and all are products of the corporate landscape of the nineties.

These shifts in corporate strategies and growth signal increased competition, and they mean the demise of the company that refuses to keep up. Mom and Pop's marmalade store "In a Jam" can make it in today's corporate world—but not only on the basis of a quality product. Pop has to be running the online storefront and working with Asian suppliers of canning products. Mom's got to be working out a trade agreement with a competitor for sharing berry shipments so extras don't spoil, and meanwhile she'll be shutting down the arm of the business that never quite caught fire—even if it means discontinuing "Aunt Betty's Broccoli Marmalade."

That's business in the future, and if you don't sometimes reinvent the wheel, you're going to spend a lot of the time by the side of the road.

I want to add two notes regarding reinventing the wheel. First, I want to be certain it's clear that I'm using the term to describe a situation in which you have a business plan, but it doesn't work for your foreign start-up. You won't know this—whether it will work or not—until you've examined it closely, and this is exactly what you need to do. Don't operate on the assumption that a business plan is a business plan is a business plan. It doesn't work that way when you're moving from a domestic to an international operation, nor does it work that way when you're moving forward at a time when technology is changing so fast that keeping up is more than a full-time job.

Companies that will flourish must adapt to the changes, and sometimes reinvent themselves in the new environment in which they find themselves. The secret lies in reinvention that is made of a combination of precision and passion.

Second, I want to comment that publicly traded companies have an additional obligation, in my opinion, to move toward greater transparency in the market. Your marketplace—your customer base—must be able to know and believe you are operating in a good-faith manner, and that your dealings are aboveboard (without fail) and predictable to the extent that they can be—meaning certain assumptions can be made about the ways in which you will do business. Your market needs to know you will not violate typical customer expectations. When this trust doesn't exist, or is damaged, it is unlikely to matter what else you do—from any standpoint.

Tip No. 3: Power

The days of the fully integrated company are fast disappearing. In many industries, they are already a piece of corporate history. I predict, based on what I have seen happening in the I.T. field, as well as in other industries, that the trend toward outsourcing and focused competency will continue, and in fact, grow. The company that grabs hold of this trend is going to be the company with power in the next millennium.

In the past we saw many more fully integrated companies, ones that were entirely self-reliant, that produced everything they needed internally and so were not a connected piece of the industry puzzle. In the days of the fully integrated company, each business was a stand-alone puzzle in and of itself. They were competition, pure and simple, but never partners in any form.

Now, with production of components coming from various sources, supplies from other sources, and services—advertising, marketing, and conference-planning, let's say—coming from yet other sources, each company relies more heavily on its outsource partners. All of the members of the supply chain take on an importance that wasn't there even five years ago in most industries. Failing to recognize this is a mistake a business without foresight will make, while the business with foresight will find itself in a position once again to move ahead of its competitors and colleagues.

From the standpoint of the customer, whether the business is fully integrated or not is of little value. The customer wants to have a relationship with the firm with which they are doing business, and they want quality, value, service, etc. The only power relevant to the customer is related to getting the product or service they want, at a price they like, when they want it. The company that can be responsive to these issues will be the company in the power position, but that has always been true, realistically. What is different, then, about power and the new millennium?

What is different is that what goes on behind the scenes is of less importance to the customer than service, price, and supply. Changes in company structure will affect every facet of the customer-supplier relationship, whether the customer is aware of it or not. Building the strongest business infrastructure from disparate parts—other suppliers, partners, and components—while maintaining that clear relationship between customer and supplier will be essential.

I am a strong proponent of the direct model, as it offers the best customer relationship. It is comprised of the customer and the company, with no in betweens. Some companies have tremendous difficulty achieving this due to their history, which may have created a huge, unwieldy system that would be nearly impossible to shift into a direct model. However, I believe those organizations that can create or approach this level of relationship will hold the power in their respective industries and emerge as winners in both the short and long run.

A typical industry model—and this spans most industries—creates multiple layers between the manufacturer and the customer; typically these layers are made up of middlemen who serve as the distributors and resellers. These models are just not as efficient, and they also serve to create distance between company and customer. Any time multiple layers are created, and any time distance is increased between the two key players in the industry game—customer and company—the power of both is diffused. No customer or company should allow itself to go in this direction.

If you think of your own experiences as a customer, regardless of the venue, you'll recognize that your power is a key part of the process and an essential element that either keeps you coming back or turns you toward another company. If your doctor makes you wait too long, you are likely to seek another doctor, unless your doctor continues to hold more power—in this case, for instance, your doctor might be the acknowledged world expert in a certain specialty within medicine, and so you may accede your wish and need for the power to control the outcome since other intrinsic rewards are involved in staying with this physician.

If your car dealer routinely keeps your car for two weeks for repairs, you're unlikely to continue to frequent that repair shop. If your grocery store promises avocados on sale but never stocks them, you will be powerless to take advantage of the benefits of the relationship, and thus you will go elsewhere. As the "provider," your company must spend considerable time and energy on power, specifically on making your customer powerful.

The way to do so is twofold. First, **create the interactional aspects of your company in the form that will best serve your customer.** As I've said, I believe that consists of a direct-model structure. The interactional aspects are the ways in which you actually deal with your customer. Second, **create your organizational infrastructure in the form that will best serve your customer.** The way to do that is to make use of the expertise, the resources, and the sources that already exist. Reinvent your company…but don't reinvent the rest of the world. Much of it is out there ready to work with you in ways that will save money, improve products and services, and give your customer what he or she wants—quality, savings, availability—without having to deal with the five or fifty sources making it possible.

So, while you are receiving the widget paint from one outsource and the boxes in which you ship the widgets from another, your customer is—and should be—only dealing with one relationship, one source, one focus of accountability: you.

In Asia, the potential for partnering has grown exponentially over the past several years—and, in fact, the potential simply wasn't there until the late nineties. Because of both the expansion of in-region business and the influx of foreign business to Asia, there are numerous new links in the supply chain, which create a tremendous supply of potential partners in many industries.

I want to back up for just a moment, though, and discuss the reasoning and logic I believe support the move away from fully integrated, stand-alone business and toward supply-chain models. I think of this theory as being about "focused competency."

Focused competency will put your company in the power position primarily because it is a reductionist theory, something extremely simple and exceedingly company friendly. Focused competency is about a business zeroing in on what it does best—and then finding experts, externally, to supply the goods and services that will allow for a continued focus on competency in that "best" area (or areas), without the distraction of having to do all of the supporting functions that make the primary competence feasible.

Let's suppose you run a hamburger stand, one known all over for creating the best hamburgers in a tristate area. Your focused competency should be making hamburgers; that's where your energy should go. You might offer french fries, milkshakes, and one or two other items, but you focus on the hamburger. In order to offer that excellent hamburger, though, you need condiments: lettuce, tomato, catsup, and mustard. You can spend your mornings tending the garden plot, the one where you grow the lettuce and tomatoes, some of which you make into catsup. You can also devote an hour or two of each weekend to making the week's stock of mustard. You dedicate Sunday evenings to cutting out squares of soft paper—these will be the napkins. Harder paper, cut into circles, will be your plates. And the utensils; I suppose you could—well, okay, so maybe you're getting the idea? For every moment you spend on the grunt work that undeniably must be done you spend one less moment making—or selling—an excellent hamburger. You're throwing away your culinary talent on kindergarten art projects, cutting out circles and squares. And for what? After all, someone else makes napkins and plates—-that's their focused competency—-and they make them well, and in such huge quantities that they can get them to you cheap and fast. The same is true with the condiments.

What focused competency also means, then, is that you need to identify and partner with those other links in the supply chain. By doing so, you will soon come to see that the alliances you create through focused competencies will come in two types: alliances with suppliers/partners, and alliances with your customers.

Supplier/Partner Alliances

I strongly believe that the companies that will wield the most power in the new world of supply-chain business are those that have clearly defined their own value in the chain while teaming with "Best in Class" partners and/or suppliers who handle the parts of the equation that are not critical for the "parent" company to own or to maintain in-house. The standard way to implement this type of partnering, of course, is outsourcing, which is when partners and suppliers remain outside of the parent company and provide the goods and services by contractual agreement, while all of the partners retain their independence and their autonomy. There are good reasons why this is the standard, not the least of which is that outsourcing maintains a separate leadership and power base (when thinking of power, it's important to remember that creating a power position isn't related solely to one's status in the industry food chain. It's also about internal organizational power; the moment your company's infrastructure weakens, your position in the food chain becomes infinitely more precarious).

Because of the benefits associated with it, outsourcing can be perceived as a "clean" process in many ways, where a price is paid for a product or service delivered, but where all of the potential "messiness" of internal corporate operations and merged administrative structures don't exist. Perhaps most important, an outsourcing model is what has typically been used in the United States. As a result, it tends to be the first model to which everyone turns when an alliance of some sort would be desirable.

In many cases, outsourcing is the preferred mode of alliance; for instance, if the product or service need is short term, it makes sense to limit the alliance to a short-term fee-for-service (or product) arrangement. It also may make sense to impose limits on the alliance created by a first-time foray into partnering with an untested outsource. This allows both parties to work out any areas needing change during the course of the limited alliance without creating a more permanent partnership prior to doing so. A longer-term outsourcing agreement can obviously follow at any point that is mutually beneficial for the partners.

The second way to implement partnering is seen less frequently—and yet I believe it is also frequently the mark of a company poised for huge growth and success. This model requires bringing suppliers and partners into the family.

Here we have another chicken-or-egg situation: Does your company wait until it's so strong that it's able to bring in partners without shaking the foundation, or do you take a leap of faith? Perhaps the best answer is both; you're not going to want to bring in multiple other suppliers if your own organizational infrastructure isn't stable. An occasional result, however, is that the added expertise, and the ability to get refocused competencies, helps to stabilize operations. These alliances require new relationship models between the partners. While they are still outsource partners—they have not been acquired and large equity stakes have not been made (in fact, on paper, they look just like the suppliers we discussed a moment ago—they have a "deep relationship" with your company.) There is connectivity of systems: Information flows are combined and shared with suppliers; planning is held jointly; and suppliers look to enable the partner rather than just seeking an opportunity for commerce. You will want to spend considerable time, for instance, on communications: Your new "family members" will need to be part of the information flow in a way that they probably are not used to with anyone else.

The attention paid to setting up communications networks and processes will pay off, the supply chain will be more streamlined, and this will lead to a better focus on competencies—which, obviously, trickles down to the customer.

Customer Alliances

I've said this a dozen different ways throughout the book, and that's because I believe it wholeheartedly: The present and future success of your company resides with the customer. I believe strongly that industry, perhaps in part because of the more anonymous nature of how business is often done now—has moved away from a customer orientation. It has become much easier to see customers in terms of market segments and in terms of numbers.

Perhaps industry has chosen to view success through these anonymous numeric systems rather than in human terms because it could be somewhat worrisome to consider the truth, the truth being that your success lies in the hands of your customer. However, that's a superficial view, because you choose how the customer will view you; you have the power, if you take it, to be a success.

As I've already discussed, the "market of one" creates a personalized focus on the individual customer, and creating an alliance with every single customer typically means creating new models of customer relations. This is how you take hold of the potential for success. Like any good model involving individuals interacting, your model of customer relations must rely heavily on communication.

Further, your model should be based on a concept I state often: Always have your customer's best interests at heart. It's easy to give this lip service. Obviously, everyone says they're customer focused; the real question is whether their actions belie their words. In truth, few companies actually follow through and see to it that customers start out satisfied and then maintain that satisfaction—and even experience an increase in it.

Ideally, your customers should be a part of your strategy and planning process all along the way in your start-up. They should also be involved in product and service development, and expansion should be customer driven. They will tell you what you need to know about any—and all—of these areas. It's actually odd that we, as business leaders, don't put our customers at the forefront of making these determinations; they are, after all, the ones who will make or break us when the product or service appears.

An added point about customer alliances: I'm sure you agree that your company should not be engaged in activities about which you wouldn't want your customers to know. I suppose this might sound heretical to those people in the corporate world who don't see customers as equal or as having the expertise or ability to truly understand the complex workings of both the business and the larger industry. (You might guess that I'm not one of those people; I think the customer can teach us more about what we should be doing—and how we should be doing it—than any other source if we listen. That's the key; we have to listen.)

The fact is many businesses don't involve customers in alliances—those close partnerships that are based on an open flow of information—because they don't want their customers to know too much. This may just be an old habit dying hard, or it may be that the company is actually conducting business in a way that wouldn't meet with the average customer's approval. This is not to say, necessarily, that such a company is behaving unethically. Many businesses operate in ways that are legal and even ethical, and all the while those ways wouldn't go over well with customers. No matter why a company attempts to retain the power base by leaving the customer out of the loop, it will ultimately lose instead, because the customer who is kept out of the flow is the customer who walks away sooner or later.

Whatever the reason for making a choice of customer avoidance over customer connection (and knowing which you're doing is well worth serious focus on your part), I wholeheartedly believe that the better you understand your customer and their needs, the better you can lead and mobilize your organization in order to satisfy them. This understanding on your part is key to supporting and serving the customer—and that, of course, is the key to organizational power and your start-up's success.

Tip No. 4: Pride

I remember taking a marketing class in college, and one of the things that we spent some time studying was how the internal structure and culture of an organization creates an external picture that makes customers more (or less) likely to trust the organization—and therefore, more (or less) likely to purchase that company's product or service. At the time we were studying this, the Xerox Corporation had redefined the entire employer-employee connection: when you were hired by Xerox, you weren't just Beth, a Xerox employee. You were a member of Team Xerox. The phrase was even spoken with emphasis, to carry the understanding that this wasn't just some marketing idea, but a real company culture and ethic. When you came to work, you were focused on being part of a "winning team," and the emphasis was on contribution and participation, rather than on individual ownership of ideas and separatist competitive approaches to success. This may sound like the most sensible thing in the world, and like something that all businesses do—no big deal—but at the time (and this wasn't so long ago!) it was a tremendous workplace innovation.

Since that time, many organizations have begun to recognize the value in creating an organizational culture that focuses on every individual worker as a valuable source of ideas and leadership; this is a shift from the more traditional workplace view, which creates divisions between those in positions of authority, who are presumed to have the ideas, and those without authority, who are expected to carry out those ideas, often blindly.

The old way, which created a one-up and one-down culture, was the antithesis of the type of culture in which employees feel pride and a sense of personal accountability.

Tip No. 4, then, is about creating organizational excellence by developing a culture that encourages personal accountability and pride in one's contributions. These two factors cannot be separated, and I believe that they are the two things that have always been present in the successful company. In an increasingly competitive business world, however, where business after business levels the playing field by competing with low prices and multiple services, these two linked facts—accountability and pride—will be the core differences that make your company achieve excellence.

In the past five to ten years, not only has the more conscious organization recognized that every employee adds value; there is also an awareness that every employee has a substantial impact on customers, either positive or negative, again regardless of the individual's level within the hierarchy. A company that does not recognize this is a company that is sending loose cannons out into the customer base and hoping there are no explosions. This seems to me to be an unrealistic hope.

Businesses have come to realize that the employee is the company in a very real sense. If a customer (or potential customer) has an unsatisfactory or unpleasant dealing with one individual employee—even if it isn't within the context or confines of the workplace—it can have reverberations throughout the entire workplace.

Disney provides an example of how organizations are redefining the role of employees and of the workplace: at the Disney theme parks, employees (called "actors") don't go to work—instead, anytime they are on the Disney property, they are "on stage."

There is no exception made for an employee on a lunch break who find himself near a guest who is lost, for instance; he is still expected to behave in a manner consistent with the Disney culture—in other words, the lunch break is delayed and the guest is helped in the friendly manner consistent with Disney's cultural ethic. The result is a consistent corporate environment that the customer has come to both expect and trust.

Imagine instead if the guest, accompanied by his young children, passed a group of costumed employees—the mouse, let's say, and Goofy—on break. Let's further suppose that the employees were enjoying their break time, relaxing by joking and laughing, loudly using swear words and calling out risque jokes. One can build an argument centered around First Amendment rights or unpaid break time or a half-dozen other points, but the bottom line is that the guest or customer is impacted by the behavior of the employees—and therefore, so is the organization. And the bottom line is all that really counts when it comes to matters of this type.

In either example, whether the employee is behaving in a manner consistent with the culture or in a manner that is damaging to the culture, the underlying key is personal accountability. A business that creates a no-defense zone in the workplace, an atmosphere where it is not all right to be closed to feedback, where it is decidedly unacceptable to respond to criticism with defensiveness, can quickly reinforce the positive behavior or eliminate the negative. The employee who offers excuses or ignores the feedback will not be able to advance in such a culture, where openness to learning is highly prized.

At Dell, defensiveness was a major sin. A company that is taking in $50 million a day on the Internet alone can't afford your hurt feelings when a supervisor suggests you stop arriving late to work. It can't afford your angry burst of temper or your peeved silence during a meeting when a colleague gives you feedback that a customer is asking to work with someone else because you often don't return that customer's calls for days or because you sound impatient when the customer asks questions. There is no time in today's business world for the little flashes of personality that we all feel the urge to share when we're criticized. Instead, we have to simply take in the feedback, recognize that it's hard to hear criticism, and **make use of that criticism anyway.**

Personal accountability involves being open to learning. If you are not only willing to hear how you can be better at whatever it is you do, but if you are also actively seeking that kind of information, you have chosen high personal accountability. You will benefit and your company will benefit. If your company is filled with people like you, people who have made the same choice, you won't be held back trying to keep employees in line, putting out fires, and cleaning up the same mistakes over and over again. All the energy that a company and individuals spend on being resistant to change and feedback could be channeled directly into the start-up and success. Seems like a no-brainer to me.

The idea behind redefining the role of the employee is based on changes in the way business is done in the nineties, changes that will continue to unfold as we enter the new millennium with all of the seen and as-yet-unseen challenges that will be a part of a new century.

I think it's important to note that many organizations have already created new terms and new paradigms for employees—just as many organizations have also created customer-friendly terms and paradigms for those with whom they do business. However, if all a company is going to do is to call an employee a team member, refer to customers as clients, or make a claim that this is a culture of accountability, the benefits aren't going to stretch very far. We've all seen companies that make a great show of lining themselves up with the next trend in corporate thinking—while at the same time these companies use the same tired customer service strategies and internal corporate behaviors they've been using all along. This type of inconsistency doesn't even have the benefit of just being neutral; it actually decreases credibility with customers, colleagues, suppliers, and employees. A company that invests heavily in clever packaging without putting anything inside the box is one that will not rate highly over the long haul.

My fourth hot tip, then, concerns how we can redefine what it means to be an employee in a company that creates the highest possible level of accountability and pride of association and ownership and participation. When employees are responsible for what they do and say, employees feel more buy-in with the outcome. This creates pride; I've seen it happen time and time again.

As for how to create such a corporate culture, you'll need to be open to all of the possible approaches, just as we discussed under the second tip, Process. You'll need to consider whether you can adapt an existing model—in this case a model of a company that creates pride by rewarding accountability and by refusing to make space for employees who are defensive and resistant to learning—or whether you'll be better off starting from scratch. Whichever you choose, don't allow yourself to be limited by what has and what hasn't been done before.

The bottom line is that you will not only want to define your company as a place employees are proud to be associated with—you'll have to be certain that your company actually lives up to this definition. Pride is hard to fake over the long haul.

Starting with the orientation you provide to your team, brainstorm and consider and reconsider everything you've done, everything you think you might want to do, and everything you've seen or heard about other companies doing—all in light of the mission and goals, and particularly as they relate to the start-up.

Your orientation, for instance, will need to cover somewhat different items with a team member who has been based at headquarters versus a team member from Asia. Both will have a different basis of experience coming into the orientation, and both will have learned different ways of looking at issues of accountability. You can begin to establish this issue as a key cultural underpinning from the earliest days, both explicitly (in company documents, in the ways you provide evaluation and supervision and the like) and implicitly (by modeling accountability in your own behavior, for instance).

You'd be amazed at how few companies provide tailored programs based on the individual shifting needs of both the company and the customer base. The employee information is more typically found in some binder designed long ago that tells you about benefits, working hours, the disciplinary policy. This is not the way to bring in leading-edge staff members, particularly not if you're after a way to bring employees on board so they develop a sense of ownership and pride in the business.

Telling people what not to do is often essential, but what gets ignored, at great cost, is the more positive approach: telling employees about how things are done in your organization.

Instead of simply focusing on bare-bones how-many-holidays types of issues, your orientation and employee manuals should include such topics (and services) as management participation, stock options, employee stock purchase plans, profit sharing, benefits, and promotion opportunities. Each of these benefits reinforces the idea of ownership, and when we own something, we tend to take better care of it—in other words, our accountability is higher. Your day-to-day corporate culture should include the equivalent of such buy-in options; your team members should be given multiple opportunities to provide leadership, feedback, and ideas, and to be a part of decision-making. Your employees should also receive ongoing feedback. By having these opportunities, employees grow in pride of ownership, and this growth only has one typical outcome: employee loyalty combined with employee excellence, and the sum of that equation is pride.

If your employees get an unmistakable sense that you're glad they're part of the organization, your employees will be glad to be part of the organization, as a rule.

The power of proud, motivated, empowered employees to create satisfied customers and to stimulate change and growth within an organization has been well documented in the leading corporations in the world—and, in fact, I'd bet that's why they're leading the world.

Like any question of how to create and run and grow a business, the question of how to approach issues of employment and benefits is one you need to address, and I'd urge you to look at this with a wide-angle lens. Look at how other corporations approach these issues. Consider what you'd like as an employee in an ideal world. Consider the idea of asking your employees what they'd most value. Also, of course, consider what's feasible, but try to remember that what results in the most savings to the company short term (such as lower pay and fewer benefits) often has the highest cost long term (in employee apathy and turnover).

Tip No. 5: Pace

As I said earlier, we are in the midst of a technology explosion that is so substantial, so fast-paced, that it has the potential to take our businesses into a realm we can't even imagine today—or to overwhelm us with the sheer volume and complexity of change if we don't approach the technology explosion with the right mind-set.

The pace at which technology is arriving and shifting will seem more manageable, less chaotic, if we can establish a set of ground rules, so to speak, for how we handle the sheer volume and speed of the innovation occurring around us. We must first understand technology: how it affects us, our customers, and our industry. Second, technology has created an open and highly competitive marketplace, and so we must establish excellence as our benchmark—nothing less. Finally, we must consider all things as possibilities: Technology gives us this potential, this gift, and if we are to not only benefit but flourish from technology, we must think in new, creative ways, ways that are not constrained by how we have approached business challenges and growth in the past.

Understanding Technology

I wholly encourage leaders and their organizations to embrace advances in technology. I'm not talking about changing infrastructure or applications every time there is a new advance, I'm talking about understanding technology.

You should understand the technological advances that have been made in the areas you currently use. Understand the new or innovative ways technologies are being used to interface with customers, suppliers, and the market, as well as what similar industries are using. Having the initiative to improve the overall understanding of technology within your organization will serve your company well.

Just as I'm not suggesting that you change at every shifting wind of technology, I'm also not recommending that everyone in your organization needs to become an I.T. specialist. However, you'll be ahead of the game if your team members have an awareness of technology that makes them ask "Is there a better way to do this?" Where companies hit obstacles is the point at which they don't know to ask.

Establish Excellence

Companies are experiencing ever-increasing drives to improve productivity, customer satisfaction, and quality, and these factors won't magically appear just by everyone working harder. Tools, whether tangible tools or process or innovation tools, will be required to continue to improve. Where in the past it may have been acceptable to just be the best within your industry, today we operate regionally or globally in the "market-space." The best in your industry is only a limited accolade.

If you are in the insurance industry and are providing the best level of customer experience, it still may not be good enough as you share your customers with the finance industry or the computer industry or the travel industry, for instance. This means that each of these other non-industry players and their activities affect your customer's level of expectation. As I speak with customers and business leaders, I hear this more and more; a customer will ask why one company can't do something they've seen another company do, even though the two organizations are in different industries. If you think about this for a moment, you may find that you do the same; your great experience at a five-star hotel may well be your new benchmark for how an airline should treat you; the recent dealings you had with a bank may be your new expectation with a telephone service provider.

We are operating in the new global market-space, and on top of that, the Internet is shredding geographic boundaries. I think this is even more important in a foreign start-up. While multiple steps and stages are involved in the start-up, you truly have only one chance to establish your company in the region, and you might as well do it right.

I have often seen companies come into a region and place facilities in every country or in multiple cities, along with manufacturing plants or warehouses, since this was the company's model in other regions of the world—the way things have always been done. Those multiple buildings could (and should) have been consolidated into just a few facilities—we know that Asia has some of the most expensive real estate and rents anywhere in the world, and applying the old procedures in this new market doesn't work as a result.

The approach you use must take into consideration your company's goals and business model. During the planning phase you have an excellent opportunity to see how the best companies do things in Asia. This will assist you in considering your goals and model, as well as your planned methods for realizing those goals and working within this model. You'll be able to see if some of the approaches used by others can be applied to your business (as an added benefit, you won't have to go through consolidations or upgrades at some point in the future, which can yield tremendous cost savings—and undoubtedly you can think of ways to put the saved time to better use!)

All Things Are Possible

Asia is a large, diverse geographical area, and I have been pleasantly surprised over the years about the assistance you can receive from firms operating within the region already. When we were first setting up the Dell business, I called many associates as well as others I did not know, and told each of them what we were going to do. I asked if our teams could meet to see if we could learn from their experiences. You might be surprised, but I was never turned down. Granted, I never asked a direct competitor, but nonetheless, the responses were open and welcoming and set the foundation for the vast majority of my experiences in Asia.

If you recall, at the beginning of this book I talked about the start-up experience as a pioneering adventure. I've often thought that the willingness to share ideas and discuss obstacles and challenges is related to the view of ourselves, our companies, and our work as occupying a pioneering place in history. Because we are all standing together at the forefront of change, perhaps there is more openness to helping each other out, less jealous guarding of secrets. It has seemed to me, at times, that this willingness to compare notes stems from the fact that we are all aware and respectful of the pioneering spirit connecting us

Over the years, after we built the Dell Asia Pacific Customer Center in Penang, Malaysia, we routinely opened our doors to others from around the region so they could learn from what we had done correctly, and from what we could have done better.

We opened it up to our customers, suppliers, other industries and governments—everyone but our direct competition, and I think you can understand why we did not do that! Our philosophy was that others had opened their doors to us, so we wanted to reciprocate with anything we could do to further promote the development of companies, governments, and the countries as a whole. As an added bonus, the sharing process served the purpose of allowing us to see our operations through fresh eyes, reeducating us about our successes and letting us see how well we were keeping pace with the rapid changes in both technology and the region. An undervalued part of the experiences with other companies was that it created goodwill, something that can't be bought no matter how long you're in a region and no matter how fast or slow you operate as a company. Goodwill is about relationships, and you can never tell when your individual and corporate goodwill is going to come back to you, and often many times over. The goodwill and success encouraged and educated me about what things are possible—and what I discovered was that almost without exception, all things are possible if approached correctly: at a reasonable pace, with the necessary supports and infrastructure in place, and with staff members who experience the pride of being part of an organization that understands that progress is based on customer-oriented processes.

Passion and Purpose

Being able to merge that which you love—-that which brings you joy, your passion—with the areas you know best technically and professionally is a gift. So many people toil at work they find dissatisfying, or worse, they spend their lives at work that limits them and slowly pulls them down into a pervasive sense of exhaustion and futility. We probably all have our moments like this, of course—-no work is without its attendant frustrations, and all work sometimes makes us wish for an escape.

It is my belief, though, that if we keep ourselves abreast of growth and change both personally and professionally, we make our days—-upon which lives are built—-an object lesson in growth and change. All work, no matter how steeped in or subject to technology, is ultimately about making the human condition better.

If we can stay in tune with this knowledge, our work becomes bigger than the sum of its parts, whether grand or mundane, and bigger than any of us or all of us who create it. Work becomes about progress and how we choose to make that progress; it becomes about the processes that allow us to bridge old borders together, borders that the Internet and other burgeoning technologies are eliminating by the minute.

Work takes on a deeper level of meaning as we experience the pride associated with being on the cusp of success, perched on the edge of the positive power of being the acknowledged industry leader.

There is more to work than even being the industry leader, though, and it is this: *How will you spend one third of your adult life? How will you spend the 100,000 work hours the average adult puts in during his or her lifetime?*

As with any effort, what we put in determines what we receive—-as well as what is available in terms of outcome. I say all of this, the summaries and the caution, because what you need is completely available to you—in your passion and in these pages.

I urge you to take the time to think not just about where you want your business to be in five or ten years, with roots put down in Asia-Pacific and elsewhere, but also about where you want to be in those years. If you're doing it right, you can't really separate the work from the person, the intention from the outcome. The result, when you invest thought and focus and energy into your work in general, and into the start-up specifically, will be a process far richer and more textured than it might have been had you approached in the old, traditional ways.

Use the principles of change and consider tips I've discussed to reach a new height both in the degree of success of your work and in your own evolution. Remember that you're on an adventure, and infuse that adventure with creativity, passion, and risk.

The result? The possibilities are endless.

A final thought:

> "The Internet is changing everything in the way we live and the way we do business. Whether these changes turn out to be a slight shuffle, or a momentous shift equivalent to an earth quake, it is up to you to determine. But one thing is for sure...
>
> The Internet is here to stay and doing nothing is no longer an option"

The Welcome Guest

When I set out to write this book, I had a rough idea of what I wanted to say. Now, at its completion, and after reading the very familiar words many times over, I am satisfied that I have said much of what was originally intended. What is striking to me, however, is how very often the subject of culture arises. I didn't set out to write a book about culture—not at all, although I anticipated addressing the issue in some depth. It occurs to me, though, having completed the book and having come to more of an awareness of just how important the idea of culture is in foreign start-up, that I owe a greater debt of gratitude to my hosts than even I knew.

Asia is, in so many ways, a magical continent. It is ancient—-and in its soil and in its soul it carries the lessons learned over many lifetimes. In comparison, so many other cultures are barely newborns; as the elder, Asia has its many lessons to offer, the wisdom of the centuries. More than just wisdom, though, there is the gracefulness and graciousness of which I've spoken. Even in its busiest provinces, its most crowded or chaotic cities, Asia and its people manage grace; surely that must be some sort of magic.

I am fortunate to have had the opportunity to live in Asia, to observe and be a part of and benefit from proximity to those graceful customs and gracious people. I have been treated kindly at every turn, and I have been made to feel less like an expatriate doing business overseas and more like a welcome guest. For that, I am indebted and grateful; my life has been changed in many ways, and made infinitely richer, because of the years I've spent here.

To my hosts, then, although no thank you could ever be adequate, for the warmth and welcome, for the gift of a home far away from home, xie xie from the bottom of my heart.

Phil Kelly,
Hong Kong
July 2000

About the Author

Phil Kelly is Founder and Chairman of NetCel360 Limited and is responsible for the company's vision, strategic direction and overall operations.

Netcel360 is Asia's first regional e-Business Service Provider (eSP), providing a comprehensive range of e-Business services to the world's leading companies operating in Asia-Pacific. Founded in 1999, NetCel360's service portfolio enables companies to gain market leadership, reduce time to market, streamline operations and focus on their core competencies. NetCel360 currently has offices in Hong Kong, Singapore, Malaysia, Japan and the United States.

Prior to establishing NetCel360, Phil served as President of Dell Computer Corporation Asia-Pacific until December 1998. He was responsible for all of Dell's business operations in the region, and for developing and implementing strategies designed to expand Dell's business in Asia-Pacific.

During his tenure at Dell, Phil opened offices and established direct operations in 11 countries and created a comprehensive distribution network across Asia-Pacific, serving customers in 49 countries. He was responsible for the establishment of Dell's 238,000-square-foot Asia

Pacific Customer Center (APCC) in Penang, Malaysia, in January 1996, that manufactures the entire line of Dell computer systems.

Under Phil's leadership, the Asia-Pacific business was recognized as Dell's fastest growing region. The organization grew to a 1,400-strong team that contributed more than US$1 billion of Dell's overall annual revenue. He was also responsible for the establishment of Dell's second Asia-Pacific manufacturing facility in Xiamen, China, which began operations in August 1998.

Prior to joining Dell, Phil was Vice President and General Manager of Motorola, Inc.'s Land Mobile Products Sector North Asia Division. Based in Hong Kong, he had complete responsibility for operations, planning, distribution and product planning for an area that included China, Hong Kong, South Korea, Taiwan, Japan, and the Philippines.

Before locating to the Asia Pacific region, Phil served as Vice President and Assistant General Manager for Motorola's Western US Division. He also held the position of vice president in charge of the Motorola Customer Response Center that established a super center for sales, engineering, finance, network management and customer service for North America. Prior to that, he created Motorola's first telephone/direct mail operation in the U.S. market.

Phil holds a Bachelor of Business Administration from the University of San Diego in the US.

A recognized spokesman for high technology and e-commerce in the Asia-Pacific region, Phil has been quoted extensively in Business Week, Fortune, Far Eastern Economic Review, the Asian Wall Street Journal as well as other various top tier Asian publications. He has appeared on CNBC and other various Asian television networks.